American
Tea Room

Cashew Salad

Page 50

Vanilla Almond
Raspberry Cake

Page 109

Our Favorite Recipes
Hand Picked For You

Printed in the United States of America
by G&R Publishing Co.

Distributed By:

CQProducts

507 Industrial Street
Waverly, IA 50677

ISBN-13: 978-1-56383-178-2
ISBN-10: 1-56383-178-3
Item #3802

Table of Contents

Cover Photo:
Kaleidoscope Inn & Gardens
Nipomo, California

Sauces & Snacks

Mullen's Irish Devonshire Cream

1 (8 oz.) pkg. cream cheese, softened
4 T. garden mint syrup (page 16)

3 T. powdered sugar
¼ C. sour cream
¼ C. heavy whipping cream

Assemble recipe with all ingredients at room temperature. In a medium mixing bowl, beat cream cheese, garden mint syrup and powdered sugar until light and fluffy. Beat in sour cream and heavy whipping cream until well blended. Refrigerate until ready to serve.

Mullen's Herbal Tea House
Barre, Massachusetts

Honey Mustard Dressing

Makes ¾ cup

2½ T. honey mustard
1 tsp. fresh grated gingerroot
2 T. red wine vinegar
1 tsp. soy sauce
1 clove garlic, finely minced

½ C. canola oil
Pinch of salt
Pepper to taste
1 T. fresh chopped chives

In a small bowl, whisk together mustard, grated gingerroot, vinegar, soy sauce and minced garlic. Slowly add oil, whisking constantly, until fully blended. Add salt, pepper and chopped chives.

The Great Galena Peddlery
Galena, Illinois

Salmon Mousse Puffs

2 (6 to 7 oz.) cans salmon, drained

½ C. butter, softened

4 oz. cream cheese, softened

3 green onions, finely chopped

3 T. dried dillweed

3 to 4 T. sour cream

2 T. lemon juice

Salt to taste

1 tube puff pastry

Preheat oven to 325°. In a blender or food processor, combine drained salmon, butter and cream cheese. Add chopped green onions and dillweed and process until just smooth. Add sour cream and lemon juice. Pulse until well blended. Season with salt and set aside. Lay out puff pastry and cut into 2½″ x 2½″ squares. Press pastry squares into the cups of a lightly greased mini muffin pan. Fill each cup with about 1½ teaspoons salmon mixture. Bake for 20 to 25 minutes.

Chantilly Tea Room & Gift Boutique
Tucson, Arizona

Chilled Fruit Cups

Makes 18 servings

1 (12 oz.) can frozen
   pineapple juice
   concentrate

1 (6 oz.) can frozen orange
   juice concentrate, thawed

1 C. water

2 T. lemon juice

3 medium firm bananas,
   sliced

1 (16 oz.) pkg. frozen
   unsweetened strawberries,
   thawed and drained

1 (15 oz.) can mandarin
   oranges, drained

1 (8 oz.) can crushed
   pineapple, drained

In a large bowl or pitcher, prepare pineapple juice according to package instructions. Add thawed orange juice concentrate, water, lemon juice, banana slices, drained strawberries, drained mandarin oranges and drained crushed pineapple. Pour ¾ cup mixture into individual containers. Cover containers and place in refrigerator until frozen. Remove from freezer 40 to 50 minutes before serving.

Swan House Tea Room & Shoppe
Findlay, Ohio

Snack Crackers

2 C. flour
6 tsp. baking powder
½ tsp. salt
1 T. sugar

½ C. butter, softened
⅓ C. milk
Salt, onion salt or garlic
    salt, optional

Preheat oven to 350°. In a large bowl, combine flour, baking powder, salt and sugar. Crumble in butter and mix with a fork. Add milk and mix until dough holds together. Roll dough to ¹/₁₆″ thickness. Cut crackers with small cookie cutters in any design. Place crackers on a greased baking sheet. Prick crackers with a fork. If desired, sprinkle lightly with salt, onion salt or garlic salt. Bake until lightly browned. At Lynn's Country Tea Place, we cut the crackers into a mini teapot shape and float on top of soup.

Lynn's Country Tea Place
Waverly, Iowa

Mini Smoked Chicken Mushroom Tarts

½ pkg. puff pastry dough, thawed

½ small red onion, thinly sliced

2 cloves garlic, minced

1 pkg. Cremini mushrooms, coarsely chopped

2 T. olive oil

1 egg

1 tsp. water

1 C. diced smoked chicken, divided

¾ C. shredded Monterey Jack cheese, divided

12 Kalamata olives, coarsely chopped, divided

1 T. finely chopped parsley, divided

1 T. finely minced scallion stems, divided

Preheat oven to 450°. Roll out pastry dough and flatten seams. Cut pastry sheet into 9 sections and place sections on a greased baking sheet. In a large pan, sauté sliced onions, minced garlic and chopped mushrooms in olive oil until softened. Remove from heat and let cool. In a small bowl, beat egg with water. Brush the borders of the pastry with egg mixture. Spread mushroom mixture into the center of each pastry section. Fold up ½" of each pastry side, pinching the corners together to hold the filling. Bake for 10 minutes. Top each tart with smoked chicken, shredded Monterey Jack cheese and chopped olives. Return to oven for an additional 10 minutes, until cheese is bubbly. Remove from oven and sprinkle each tart with chopped parsley and scallions. Serve warm.

The Great Galena Peddlery
Galena, Illinois

Salmon & Lemon Kisses

1¼ C. flour
½ tsp. baking powder
1 T. fresh chopped parsley
1 (6 to 7 oz.) can salmon, drained
1 oz. smoked salmon (nova lox)

½ tsp. liquid smoke
1 T. lemon juice
6 T. butter, softened
4 oz. cream cheese, softened
1 egg

Preheat oven to 325°. Line baking sheets with parchment paper. In a large bowl, combine flour and baking powder. Using a hand mixer, mix in chopped parsley, drained salmon, smoked salmon, liquid smoke, lemon juice, butter, cream cheese and egg. When dough is blended, spoon mixture into a pastry bag. Using your choice of tips, squeeze out kisses onto lined baking sheets about 1½″ apart. Bake for 20 minutes. The baked and cooled kisses can be frozen up to 3 months.

Chantilly Tea Room & Gift Boutique
Tucson, Arizona

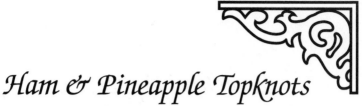

Ham & Pineapple Topknots

Makes 4 servings

4 ham steaks

4 crumpets

½ C. shredded English
  Cheddar cheese

½ tsp. dry mustard

2 tsp. milk

4 pineapple rings

Watercress for garnish,
  optional

Preheat grill. Slowly cook ham steaks over grill. Toast crumpets over grill or in a broiler. In a medium bowl, combine shredded English Cheddar cheese, dry mustard and milk. Spread mixture over tops of toasted crumpets and grill until golden brown. Place grilled ham steaks over toasted filling on crumpets and top with a pineapple ring. Grill until thoroughly heated, being careful not to burn. If desired, garnish with watercress.

The Front Parlour Tearoom at The British Shoppe
Madison, Connecticut

Zucchini Appetizers

3 C. shredded zucchini
1 C. Bisquick baking mix
½ C. chopped onion
½ C. grated Parmesan cheese
2 tsp. fresh diced parsley
½ tsp. salt
½ tsp. dried oregano
1 clove garlic, minced
½ C. oil
4 eggs, slightly beaten

Preheat oven to 350°. In a lightly greased 9 x 13″ baking dish, combine shredded zucchini, Bisquick, chopped onions, grated Parmesan cheese, diced parsley, salt, dried oregano, minced garlic, oil and beaten eggs. Mix until evenly blended. Bake for 25 minutes, until golden brown. Cut into small squares before serving.

A Perfect Blend
Lititz, Pennsylvania

Pomegranate Walnut Baklava

2 C. honey
2 (15 oz.) jars pomegranate juice
2 lbs. chopped walnuts
2 T. cinnamon
1 tsp. nutmeg
1 tsp. ground cloves
1 box phyllo dough, thawed
Clarified butter, melted

Preheat oven to 350°. In a large saucepan over medium heat, combine honey and pomegranate juice. Reduce liquid until mixture resembles molasses. Remove from heat and mix in chopped walnuts, cinnamon, nutmeg and ground cloves. To assemble baklava, place six of the phyllo sheets on a flat surface. Place a lightly greased 9 x 13″ pan over sheets and trace around the edge of pan using a sharp knife, assuring cut phyllo rectangles will fit inside pan. Place 1 cut phyllo sheet inside pan and brush lightly with melted butter. Repeat with other 5 cut phyllo sheets, spreading butter between each layer. Arrange half of the pomegranate and walnut mixture evenly over dough in pan. Cut another 6 sheets phyllo dough to fit pan. Layer sheets in pan, 1 at a time, brushing melted butter between each layer. Top with remaining half of the pomegranate and walnut mixture and top with another 6 cut phyllo sheets, spreading melted butter between each layer. Bake for about 40 minutes, until golden brown.

Aion Antiquities & Tea House
Chicago, Illinois

Cherry Tomato Bites

2 pints cherry tomatoes
1 (8 oz.) pkg. cream cheese,
  softened
2 to 4 slices bacon, cooked
  and crumbled

¼ C. minced green onions
¼ C. fresh minced parsley
¼ tsp. Worcestershire sauce

Cut a thin slice off the top of each tomato. Carefully scoop out and discard pulp. Invert the tomatoes onto a paper towel to drain. In a small bowl, combine cream cheese, crumbled bacon, green onions, minced parsley and Worcestershire sauce. Mix well. Spoon mixture into tomatoes. Refrigerate until serving. If desired, garnish with parsley sprigs.

Tale of Two Sisters Tearoom & Gift Shoppe
Red Wing, Minnesota

Artichoke Purses

¼ C. mayonnaise
¼ C. cream cheese, softened
¼ C. shredded mozzarella cheese
⅛ C. grated Parmesan cheese
¼ C. chopped artichoke hearts
½ tsp. minced garlic

¼ onion, finely chopped
1 tsp. fresh finely chopped basil
1 scallion, finely chopped
Pinch of pepper
1 tube puff pastry

Preheat oven to 375°. In a large bowl, combine mayonnaise, cream cheese, shredded mozzarella cheese, grated Parmesan cheese, chopped artichoke hearts, minced garlic, finely chopped onion, chopped basil, finely chopped scallion and pepper. Cut puff pastry sheets into 3″ squares and place on a lightly greased baking sheet. Place 1½ tablespoons of the filling in the middle of each pastry square. Pull up the four corners of each pastry square and twist at the top to seal the filling. Bake for 10 to 20 minutes.

Boulder Dushanbe Teahouse
Boulder, Colorado

Ham & Pepper Jack Rolls

Makes 48 servings

2 C. flour

2 tsp. baking powder

½ tsp. baking soda

½ tsp. salt

½ tsp. sugar

½ C. butter

¾ C. buttermilk

4 T. Dijon mustard, divided

4 T. honey, divided

1 lb. thinly sliced deli ham, divided

¼ lb. sliced Pepper Jack cheese, cut into ½" strips, divided

Preheat oven to 350°. Grease two miniature muffin tins with non-stick spray. In a mixing bowl, combine flour, baking powder, baking soda, salt and sugar. Cut in butter and stir in buttermilk until just combined. Turn dough onto a floured surface and shape into a disk; cut into four equal pieces and set aside for 5 minutes. Roll one piece of dough into a 6 x 14" rectangle; spread with 1 tablespoon mustard and 1 tablespoon honey. Top with ¼ of the ham and two rows of cheese strips, placed about 1½" apart. Roll, jellyroll style, into a 14" long strip; cut into 12 slices. Place one roll in each mini muffin cup. Repeat with remaining dough, mustard, honey, ham and cheese to make 48 total pieces. Bake for 7 to 10 minutes or until barely golden. Serve warm or cool and freeze until needed.

Use this same method to make delicious mini Cinnamon Rolls. Just double the sugar in the dough, then sprinkle cinnamon and sugar over the dough; roll and bake as described above. If desired, drizzle warm rolls with a glaze made from softened butter, powdered sugar and warm water.

**The Secret Garden Tea Room
Sumner, Washington**

Roasted Red Pepper Pesto Pinwheels

4 tsp. minced garlic
½ C. walnuts
1 (14 oz.) can roasted red peppers, partially drained
2 oz. olive oil

1 C. grated Parmesan cheese
Salt and pepper to taste
Cream cheese, softened
Spinach tortillas

In a blender or food processor, process garlic and walnuts until finely chopped. Add roasted red peppers with some juice, olive oil, grated Parmesan cheese, salt and pepper. Process until smooth and thick enough to spread. Adjust consistency, if necessary, by adding more nuts to thicken or more oil to thin. Spread a layer of cream cheese over each spinach tortilla. Spread a thin layer of walnut mixture (pesto) over cream cheese. Roll tortilla as tightly as possible. Refrigerate tortillas for 30 minutes. Slice each tortilla into 1″ thick pinwheels.

Chantilly Tea Room & Gift Boutique
Tucson, Arizona

Garden Mint Syrup

¾ C. fresh mint leaves   **2 C. sugar**
1 C. water

Crush mint leaves and place in a medium saucepan. Add water and sugar to saucepan and bring to a boil over medium heat. Mix until sugar is dissolved. Reduce heat to low and let simmer for 8 to 10 minutes. Strain mixture into a bottle and refrigerate until ready to serve. Serve over pancake, waffles or use in Mullen's Irish Devonshire Cream recipe (page 2).

Mullen's Herbal Tea House
Barre, Massachusetts

Flap Jacks

1½ C. margarine **5 T. corn syrup**
1½ C. sugar **7 C. old fashioned oats**

Preheat oven to 350°. Lightly grease a baking sheet and set aside. In a medium saucepan over low heat, combine margarine, sugar and corn syrup. Cook, stirring occasionally, until melted. Remove from heat and stir in oats, mixing until well blended. Spread mixture onto prepared baking sheet and flatten with the back of a spoon. Bake for 25 minutes, until evenly browned. Remove from oven and let set for a few minutes before cutting into 1″ x 2″ fingers. Let cool completely, remove from baking sheet and store in an airtight container.

Lady Caroline's British Tea Shop
Omaha, Nebraska

Spinach & Cheese Savory

1 lb. frozen chopped spinach, thawed and drained

1 C. cottage cheese

½ C. grated Parmesan cheese

½ C. crumbled feta cheese

1 T. fresh chopped dill

2 tsp. garlic pepper

4 extra large eggs, beaten

1 pkg. frozen puff pastry

Preheat oven to 375°. In a large bowl, combine drained spinach, cottage cheese, grated Parmesan cheese, crumbled feta cheese, fresh chopped dill, garlic pepper and beaten eggs. Mix until well blended. Spread out frozen puff pastry squares. Place ¼ cup spinach mixture in the center of each square. Fold pastry over and seal pastry by pressing down with a fork. Bake according to puff pastry package directions.

The Gilded Rose Manor
Northridge, California

Breads & Sides

Savory Cheese Scones

3 C. self-rising flour
1 T. baking powder
¼ tsp. salt
1 tsp. dried parsley flakes
1 tsp. Italian seasoning
1 tsp. garlic powder

10 T. butter, softened, divided
½ C. shredded Cheddar cheese
¾ C. cold buttermilk

Preheat oven to 450°. In a large bowl, thoroughly combine self-rising flour, baking powder, salt, parsley flakes, Italian seasoning and garlic powder. Using a pastry blender, cut in 8 tablespoons butter until combined and mixture is crumbly. Stir in shredded Cheddar cheese. Form a well in the center of the mixture and pour buttermilk into well, stirring to combine. Turn dough out onto a flat floured surface and knead dough for about 1 minute. Using hands, pat out dough to ½" thickness. Cut dough with a 1" biscuit cutter. Place scones on a lightly greased baking sheet. Bake for about 8 minutes. Melt remaining 2 tablespoons butter and brush melted butter over warm scones.

the shoppe at Shady Gables
Authentic English Tearoom and Gift Gallery
Versailles, Missouri

Retro Rosemary Scones

Makes 12 to 15 scones

2 tsp. finely minced fresh rosemary

½ C. butter, softened

1¾ C. unbleached flour

⅔ C. old fashioned or quick oats

1 T. baking powder

¼ tsp. salt

2 eggs, beaten

⅓ C. half n' half or 2% milk

½ C. plus 2 T. shredded Cheddar cheese, divided

Mince rosemary as finely as possible and mix with butter in a small bowl. Cover and refrigerate overnight. Preheat oven to 400°. In a medium bowl, combine flour, oats, baking powder and salt. Cut rosemary butter into dry ingredients using a pastry blender or mixer on a low setting, until mixture resembles cornmeal. Add beaten eggs and enough half n' half to make a firm dough. Mix in ½ cup shredded Cheddar cheese and transfer dough to a flat, lightly floured surface. Knead dough and press or roll to ½″ thickness. Cut scones with a biscuit cutter or knife. Place scones on an ungreased baking sheet and sprinkle tops of scones with remaining 2 tablespoons shredded Cheddar cheese. Bake for 10 to 12 minutes, until golden brown. Transfer to a wire rack to cool slightly. Serve warm.

Retro Tea Room
Bowie, Maryland

Cranberry Scones

Makes 2 dozen

4 C. flour
2 T. baking powder
4 T. sugar
1 tsp. salt

½ C. butter or margarine, softened
1 C. milk or buttermilk
2 to 3 C. dried cranberries or craisins

Preheat oven to 325°. In a large bowl, combine flour, baking powder, sugar and salt, mixing until blended. Add butter and milk. Mix until dough clings together and is a bit sticky. Fold in dried cranberries, being careful to handle dough as little as possible. Over handling will cause scones to be hard. Roll dough out on a floured cutting board and cut with a round cookie cutter. Place scones on a greased baking sheet. Bake for 18 minutes, until lightly browned.

Variation: To make shiny brown scones, brush the top of each scone with a lightly beaten egg before baking.

Elise's Tea Room
Long Beach, California

Rosalyn Carter's Scones

3 C. self-rising flour
¾ T. cinnamon
½ C. sugar
½ C. butter, softened

1 C. buttermilk
¼ C. raisins
Egg whites

Preheat oven to 400°. In a large bowl, combine flour, cinnamon and sugar. Using a pastry blender, cut in butter until mixture is crumbly. Add buttermilk and raisins, mixing until dough is soft. Turn dough out onto a flat floured surface and pat to ½″ thickness. Cut scones with a round biscuit cutter and place on a greased baking sheet. Brush tops of scones with egg whites. Bake until lightly browned.

Magnolia & Ivy
Destin, Florida

The Little Café & Tea Shoppe's Famous English Scones

4 C. flour
1 C. sugar
1½ tsp. baking soda
3 tsp. cream of tartar
¼ T. salt

1 C. unsalted butter, softened
1 C. craisins, optional
2 eggs, beaten
Buttermilk

Preheat oven to 425°. Into a large bowl, sift flour, sugar, baking soda, cream of tartar and salt. Sift entire mixture twice. Using a pastry blender, cut in butter. If desired, stir in craisins. Add beaten eggs and mix until thoroughly blended. Add enough buttermilk to make mixture easy to blend, but stiff. On a flat floured surface, roll out dough to 1½″ thickness. Cut scones using a 2″ biscuit cutter. Place scones on greased and lined baking sheets. Bake in oven until golden brown. If desired, serve with Devonshire cream and your favorite preserves.

The Little Café & Tea Shoppe
Jupiter, Florida

Strawberry Muffins

4 T. butter, softened
1 C. sugar
2 eggs
1 C. milk
1 C. flour

1 T. vanilla
½ T. baking powder
1½ oz. strawberry flavored
  gelatin

Preheat oven to 350°. In a large bowl, cream butter and sugar together. Add eggs, one at a time, and blend well. Mix in milk, flour, vanilla, baking powder and strawberry gelatin. Mix for 2 minutes, until batter is smooth. Pour batter into greased muffin tins, filling each cup ¾ full. Bake for 20 to 25 minutes.

A Spot For Tea
Oklahoma City, Oklahoma

Cranberry Cream Cheese Muffins

Makes 1½ dozen

1 C. butter, softened
8 oz. cream cheese, softened
1½ C. sugar
1½ tsp. vanilla
4 eggs
2 C. flour

1½ tsp. baking powder
½ tsp. salt
2 C. chopped fresh
  or frozen cranberries
½ C. chopped walnuts,
  optional

Preheat oven to 350°. Grease the cups of a muffin tin and set aside. In a large bowl, cream together butter, cream cheese, sugar and vanilla. Add eggs, one at a time, beating well after each addition. Add flour, baking powder and salt. Fold in chopped cranberries and walnuts. Spoon batter into prepared muffin tins. Bake for 25 to 30 minutes.

The Rose Cottage Gift Shop & Tea Room
Clear Lake, Iowa

Raisin Tea Bread

Makes 2 loaves

2½ C. flour	¾ C. milk
2 tsp. baking powder	½ C. olive oil
Pinch of salt	½ C. raisins
1 C. sugar	Grated zest of 1 lemon
2 eggs, lightly beaten	

Preheat oven to 350°. In a medium mixing bowl, combine flour, baking soda, salt and sugar. Add beaten eggs, milk and olive oil. Toss raisins with a little flour. Add to batter along with grated lemon zest. Stir until well combined. Grease 2 loaf pans. Pour batter into prepared pans. Bake for 15 minutes.

Christine's B&B and Tea Room
Great Barrington/Housatonic, Massachusetts

Buttermilk Chocolate Bread

Makes 1 loaf

1 C. sugar
½ C. butter, softened
2 eggs
1 C. buttermilk
1¾ C. flour

½ C. cocoa powder
½ tsp. baking powder
½ tsp. baking soda
½ tsp. salt

Preheat oven to 350°. Grease the bottom of a 5 x 9″ loaf pan and set aside. In a large bowl, combine sugar and butter until well blended. Add eggs and beat well. Stir in buttermilk, flour, cocoa powder, baking powder, baking soda and salt. Stir just until dry ingredients are moistened. Pour batter into prepared pan. Bake for 55 to 60 minutes or until a toothpick inserted in center comes out clean. Let cool for 15 minutes before removing from pan. Cool 1 hour and wrap tightly with plastic wrap. Store in refrigerator.

Chantilly Tea Room & Gift Boutique
Tucson, Arizona

Lemon-Blueberry Bread

Makes 1 loaf

1¼ C. sugar, divided
½ C. milk
½ C. unsalted butter,
  softened, divided
1 egg
2⅓ C. flour, divided

2 tsp. baking powder
¼ tsp. salt
2 C. fresh blueberries
1 T. plus 1 tsp. grated
  lemon peel
½ tsp. cinnamon

Preheat oven to 375°. In a medium bowl, combine ¾ cup sugar, milk, ¼ cup butter and egg, mixing until smooth. In a separate bowl, combine 2 cups flour, baking powder and salt. Mix well and add to sugar mixture. Fold in blueberries and 1 tablespoon grated lemon peel. Pour mixture into a greased 5 x 9″ loaf pan. To make topping, in a small bowl, combine remaining ½ cup sugar, remaining ⅓ cup flour, remaining ¼ cup butter, remaining 1 teaspoon grated lemon peel and cinnamon. Mix well and sprinkle over batter in pan. Bake for 50 minutes, until topping is golden brown and crusty. Remove from oven and cool on a wire rack.

The Wenham Tea House and Shops
Wenham, Massachusetts

Irish Soda Bread

Makes 3 loaves

7 C. flour	½ C. butter, softened
1 C. medium rye flour	1½ C. raisins
½ C. sugar	4 T. caraway seeds
2 tsp. salt	1 qt. buttermilk
2 tsp. baking soda	or whole milk
4 tsp. baking powder	

Preheat oven to 365°. Grease and flour three 8½ x 4" loaf pans and set aside. In a large bowl, combine flour, medium rye flour, sugar, salt, baking soda and baking powder. Add butter, stirring until just mixed. Stir in raisins and caraway seeds. Add buttermilk and stir until just mixed. Dough should be sticky. Drop batter into prepared pans. Bake for 45 to 50 minutes or until a toothpick inserted in the center comes out clean.

Sheffield's Tea Room
Wallace, North Carolina

Mango Bread

Makes 1 loaf

2 C. flour
2 tsp. baking soda
2 tsp. cinnamon
½ tsp. salt
3 eggs, well beaten

1½ C. sugar
⅔ C. oil
1½ C. chopped mangos
½ C. chopped nuts or raisins

Preheat oven to 350°. In a large bowl, combine flour, baking soda, cinnamon and salt. Mix until blended and form a well in center of mixture. Pour in beaten eggs, sugar, oil, chopped mangos and chopped nuts or raisins. Mix well and pour into a greased 5 x 9″ loaf pan. Bake for 1 hour.

Rose Mountain Manor B&B and Tea Room
Colfax, California

Zucchini Orange Bread

Makes 2 loaves

4 eggs	**1½ tsp. baking powder**
1½ C. sugar	**1½ tsp. baking soda**
¾ C. oil	**1 tsp. salt**
⅔ C. orange juice	**2½ tsp. cinnamon**
2 C. shredded zucchini	**½ tsp. ground cloves**
3¼ C. flour	**2 tsp. grated orange peel**

Preheat oven to 350°. Grease and flour two 8 x 4″ loaf pans. Parchment paper may be added to the bottom of the loaf pans. In a large bowl, beat eggs until thick and lemon colored. Gradually beat in sugar. Stir in oil, orange juice, shredded zucchini, flour, baking powder, baking soda, salt, cinnamon, ground cloves and grated orange peel. Mix until well blended. Pour batter into prepared pans. Bake for 45 to 55 minutes. Let cool for 10 minutes and remove from pans. Cool on wire racks.

Tale of Two Sisters Tearoom & Gift Shoppe
Red Wing, Minnesota

Strawberry Tea Bread

Makes 1 loaf

½ C. butter, softened
1 C. sugar
½ tsp. almond extract
2 eggs, separated
2 C. flour

1 tsp. baking powder
1 tsp. baking soda
1 (10 oz.) pkg. frozen
   strawberries, thawed

Preheat oven to 350°. Lightly grease a 5 x 9″ loaf pan and set aside. In a large bowl, cream together butter, sugar and almond extract. Add egg yolks to butter mixture, one at a time, until light and fluffy. Sift in flour, baking powder and baking soda and mix well. Drain juice from strawberries, reserving ¼ cup juice. Add reserved ¼ cup juice to mixture and fold in drained strawberries. In a separate bowl, beat egg whites to stiff peaks. Fold egg whites into mixture and pour mixture into prepared pan. Lightly drop pan to release any air bubbles. Bake for 50 to 60 minutes or until a toothpick inserted in center comes out clean. Let bread cool before slicing.

Rose Mountain Manor B&B and Tea Room
Colfax, California

Mandelbrot

Makes 2 or 3 loaves

¼ lb. butter or margarine, softened

1½ C. sugar

3 eggs

2 tsp. baking powder

2½ C. flour

6 oz. chocolate chips

1 C. chopped and pitted dates

1 C. chopped walnuts, or other nuts

Preheat oven to 375°. In a medium bowl, cream butter with sugar. Add eggs, baking powder and flour. Blend mixture into a stiff dough. Add chocolate chips, chopped dates and nuts. Drop dough lengthwise onto an ungreased jellyroll pan or baking sheet, forming logs. Be careful not to drop dough too close to edges as it will spread a lot. Can make 2 wider or 3 narrow logs. Pat logs along sides and tops to make even. Bake for 20 to 30 minutes, until deep golden brown, being careful not to burn edges. Remove from oven. Using a greased knife, immediately cut logs into slices crosswise. The Mandelbrot will be moist but the slices will harden and crisp as they cool. Using a spatula, carefully remove slices from pan while hot and let cool on a wire rack.

Noted: A cinnamon and sugar mixture may be sprinkled on top of logs before baking. Recipe may be doubled or tripled and freezes well.

Christine's B&B and Tea Room
Great Barrington/Housatonic, Massachusetts

Frozen Cranberry Salad

8 oz. cream cheese, softened
½ C. mayonnaise
1 C. sugar

2 (12 oz.) cans cranberry sauce
2 C. heavy whipping cream
1 C. powdered sugar

In a large mixing bowl, combine cream cheese, mayonnaise and sugar using the whip attachment on mixer, until smooth. Add cranberry sauce and continue mixing until smooth. In a separate bowl, combine heavy cream and powdered sugar and whip to medium stiff peaks. Fold whipped cream mixture into cranberry mixture until fully combined. Scoop cranberry salad into individual cups and place in freezer for 1 hour, until frozen. Serve chilled.

A Spot For Tea
Oklahoma City, Oklahoma

Mandarin Rice Salad

1 C. wild rice
1 C. mandarin oranges
¼ C. chopped green onions
½ C. dried cranberries
¼ C. pecans, toasted*

¼ C. fresh chopped mint leaves
½ C. orange juice
¼ C. oil
1 tsp. salt
Pinch of pepper

Cook wild rice according to package directions. In a large bowl, toss together cooked wild rice, mandarin oranges, chopped green onions, dried cranberries, toasted pecans and chopped mint leaves. In a small bowl, combine orange juice, oil, salt and pepper. Pour orange juice mixture over wild rice mixture. Toss until evenly coated. Let sit at room temperature at least 2 hours before serving.

To toast, place pecans in a single layer on a baking sheet. Bake at 350° for approximately 10 minutes or until nuts are golden brown.

An Afternoon to Remember – Tea Parlor and Gifts
Newcastle, California

Sun-Dried Tomato & Spinach Bowtie Pasta Salad

Makes 4 to 6 servings

1 lb. uncooked bowtie pasta

3 green onions, finely chopped

2 oz. sun-dried tomatoes, cut into strips

1 lb. spinach, trimmed and shredded

⅓ C. pine nuts, toasted*

1 T. dried oregano

1 tsp. salt

¾ C. grated Parmesan cheese, divided

3 T. olive oil

1 to 2 tsp. crushed red pepper

1 clove garlic, minced

Salt and pepper to taste

In a large pan of boiling water, cook bowtie pasta. Drain well and rinse under cold water. Transfer drained pasta to a large salad bowl. Add finely chopped green onions, sun-dried tomatoes, spinach, toasted pine nuts, oregano, salt and ½ cup grated Parmesan cheese. To make dressing, in a small jar with a lid, combine olive oil, crushed red pepper, minced garlic, salt and pepper. Shake well. Pour dressing over salad and toss until evenly coated. Before serving, sprinkle salad with remaining ¼ cup grated Parmesan cheese.

To toast, place pine nuts in a single layer on a baking sheet. Bake at 350 for approximately 10 minutes or until pine nuts are golden brown.*

Chantilly Tea Room & Gift Boutique
Tucson, Arizona

Sausage Rolls

2 sheets flaky puff pastry
12 pork sausage links

Egg wash for glaze (egg mixed with a bit of water)

Preheat oven to 375°. Cut sausage links apart and lay, end to end, 1″ from the side of 1 puff pastry sheet. Fold the edge of the puff pastry up and over sausages, overlapping ½″ on the other side of the sausage. Cut long roll of sausage from pastry and press cut edge with a fork to enclose. Cut into 1″ sections and place individual sausage rolls on a lightly greased baking sheet. Continue with remaining sausages and puff pastry. Glaze sausage rolls with egg wash. Bake for 25 minutes, until golden brown. Tip baking sheet to allow grease to run away from sausage rolls. Place rolls on paper towels to drain. Serve warm.

Lady Caroline's British Tea Shop
Omaha, Nebraska

Forbidden Rice

1 C. Chinese Forbidden
    Black rice
3 C. water
1 sprig fresh parsley,
    chopped
¼ C. chopped walnuts

¼ C. crumbled blue cheese
2 tsp. balsamic dressing
2 tsp. olive oil
Pinch of brown sugar
1 Asian or Bosc pear, sliced
    thin length-wise

In a medium saucepan, combine rice and water. Cover pan and let boil for 30 minutes. Remove from heat, drain rice and let cool. In a large bowl, toss together cooled rice, chopped parsley, chopped walnuts, crumbled blue cheese, balsamic dressing, olive oil and brown sugar. Mix until evenly incorporated. Chill in refrigerator until ready to serve. Before serving, garnish rice with fresh pear slices.

Aion Antiquities & Tea House
Chicago, Illinois

Roasted Corn Polenta

Makes 8 servings

2 cloves garlic, minced

2 T. olive oil

2 C. fresh or frozen corn
   kernels

1½ C. milk

1½ C. chicken broth

2 T. butter

Pepper to taste

1 C. polenta

1 C. grated Parmesan cheese

Flour for dusting

In a medium skillet over medium heat, sauté minced garlic in olive oil for 1 minute. Add corn and sauté until corn starts to brown. Remove from heat and let cool. In a large saucepan, combine milk, chicken broth, butter and pepper. Bring mixture to a boil. Add polenta, whisking constantly. Reduce heat and let mixture simmer, stirring constantly, until polenta pulls away from sides of pan, about 5 minutes. Stir in corn mixture and grated Parmesan cheese. Place mixture in a greased long rectangular pan. Cover with plastic wrap and chill in refrigerator for 3 to 4 hours. Remove polenta from pan and cut into 16 triangles. Dust each triangle with flour. Brown polenta triangles on a lightly greased griddle or skillet until crusty and heated throughout.

The Great Galena Peddlery
Galena, Illinois

Stuffed French Toast

Makes 12 servings

1 loaf raisin bread	**8 eggs**
1 (8 oz.) pkg. cream cheese	**1 C. maple syrup, divided**
2½ C. milk	**½ C. butter, melted**

Grease a 9 x 13″ baking dish. Cube raisin bread and place half of the bread cubes in bottom of prepared dish. Slice cream cheese into pieces and layer over bread cubes in dish. Top with remaining half of bread cubes. In a medium bowl, combine milk, eggs and ½ cup maple syrup. Pour mixture completely over bread cubes in pan. Chill in refrigerator overnight. Preheat oven to 350°. Bake for 1 hour. In a separate bowl, combine remaining ½ cup maple syrup and melted butter. Before serving, pour syrup mixture over French toast.

Rose Mountain Manor B&B and Tea Room
Colfax, California

Salmon Asparagus Tart

Makes 6 servings

1 lb. asparagus, trimmed and cut into 2″ pieces

¼ C. chopped onion

¼ C. sweet red or yellow peppers

2 T. butter

4 oz. cream cheese, softened

½ C. mayonnaise

2 T. flour

2 eggs, beaten

½ C. half n' half

1 tsp. dried dillweed

½ tsp. dried basil

¼ tsp. pepper

1 (15 oz.) can de-boned salmon, drained

2 C. shredded Swiss cheese

2 T. grated Parmesan cheese

Preheat oven to 350°. In a medium saucepan, bring 1″ water to a boil. Place asparagus in a steamer basket over water, cover and let steam for 4 to 5 minutes, until crisp but tender. Drain asparagus. In a skillet, sauté onion and peppers in butter until tender. In a medium mixing bowl, combine cream cheese, mayonnaise, flour, beaten eggs, half n' half, dried dillweed, dried basil and pepper. Fold in drained salmon, steamed asparagus, onion mixture and shredded Swiss cheese. Transfer to a greased 9″ pie plate. Sprinkle grated Parmesan cheese over top. Bake for 35 minutes or until a knife inserted in center comes out clean.

Lynn's Country Tea Place
Waverly, Iowa

43

Scrambled Eggs Alfredo Bake

Makes 6 servings

1 C. Bisquick baking mix
¼ tsp. Italian seasoning
6 T. butter or margarine, softened, divided
13 eggs, divided
¼ C. chopped onion

¼ C. chopped green bell pepper
1 (4½ oz.) can sliced mushrooms, drained
⅓ C. crumbled cooked bacon
¾ C. Alfredo pasta sauce

Preheat oven to 400°. Grease an 8 x 8″ baking dish and set aside. In a small bowl, combine Bisquick, Italian seasoning and 4 tablespoons butter with a pastry blender until mixture is crumbly. Gently stir in 1 egg and set aside. In a medium skillet over medium heat, melt remaining 2 tablespoons butter. Sauté onion, pepper and mushrooms in skillet for about 3 to 5 minutes, stirring occasionally, until vegetables are tender but crisp. Add remaining 12 eggs, stirring occasionally, until eggs are set. Remove from heat and stir in crumbled cooked bacon and Alfredo sauce. Spread mixture into prepared baking dish. Sprinkle Bisquick mixture over egg mixture in pan. Bake for about 15 minutes, until topping is golden brown.

Rose Mountain Manor B&B and Tea Room
Colfax, California

Canadian Bacon Quiche

4 eggs

2 C. half n' half

1 tomato, chopped

1 C. diced Canadian bacon

½ C. smoked Gouda cheese

1 tsp. garlic salt

1 tsp. pepper

1 tsp. dried basil

1 (9") unbaked pie crust

Preheat oven to 325°. In a large bowl, combine eggs, half n' half, chopped tomatoes, diced Canadian bacon, Gouda cheese, garlic salt, pepper and dried basil. Mix well and pour mixture into unbaked pie crust. Bake for 45 to 60 minutes.

A Spot For Tea
Oklahoma City, Oklahoma

Asparagus Frittata

Makes 6 servings

12 fresh asparagus spears
1 T. extra light olive oil
1 clove garlic, minced
15 eggs
¼ C. whole milk

¼ C. shredded Cheddar cheese
¼ C. shredded Monterey Jack cheese
1 tsp. seasoning salt

Wash and chop asparagus spears into approximately 1″ pieces. In a 9″ frying pan, heat olive oil and add asparagus and minced garlic. Sauté over medium heat until asparagus is slightly tender. Into a large bowl, combine eggs and milk, beating until well combined. Pour egg mixture into frying pan and add shredded Cheddar cheese, shredded Monterey Jack cheese and seasoning salt. Mix well, cover and place over medium heat for a few minutes. Remove cover and stir well. Reduce heat to low and replace cover. Once most of the eggs have solidified, cut frittata into 6 slices and carefully flip each slice over in the pan. Cook for an additional 2 to 3 minutes before serving.

Kaleidoscope Inn & Gardens
Nipomo, California

Crustless Quiche

¾ C. flour
1 tsp. baking powder
1 tsp. salt
½ tsp. dried dillweed
½ tsp. nutmeg
1 T. dried onion

1 lb. shredded Monterey
 Jack cheese
10 oz. fresh spinach
1 C. milk
3 eggs, beaten
¼ C. butter, melted

Preheat oven to 350°. In a large bowl, combine flour, baking powder, salt, dried dillweed, nutmeg and dried onion. Add shredded Monterey Jack cheese and fresh spinach. Mix until evenly coated. In a medium bowl, combine milk, beaten eggs and melted butter. Pour over dry ingredients and mix until well blended. Pour mixture into a greased 9 x 13″ baking dish. Bake for 20 to 30 minutes.

British Pantry & Tea Garden Café
Tecumseh, Michigan

Vegetable Quiche

8 to 10 oz. frozen broccoli or chopped spinach, thawed and drained
2 C. shredded Cheddar cheese
½ C. chopped green onions
¼ C. chopped red bell pepper

4 eggs
2 C. milk
1 C. Bisquick baking mix
½ tsp. salt
¼ tsp. pepper

Preheat oven to 400°. Lightly grease a 9″ or 10″ pie pan. Layer drained broccoli or spinach in bottom of prepared pan. Cover with shredded Cheddar cheese, chopped green onions and chopped red pepper. In a blender or food processor, combine eggs, milk, Bisquick, salt and pepper. Mix until thoroughly blended. Pour mixture over ingredients in pie pan. Bake for 40 minutes, until quiche is set.

Rose Mountain Manor B&B and Tea Room
Colfax, California

Miss Ruby's Chicken Salad

5 skinless, boneless chicken breast halves
3 stalks celery, diced
1 C. mayonnaise
2½ tsp. tarragon

½ tsp. salt
⅛ tsp. pepper
2 tsp. cider vinegar
2 tsp. sugar

In a large pot of water, boil chicken. Dice or shred chicken and place in a medium bowl. Add diced celery. In a small bowl, combine mayonnaise, tarragon, salt, pepper, cider vinegar and sugar. Add mayonnaise mixture to chicken and celery. Mix until evenly coated. Serve plain or as a sandwich with bread or croissants.

Miss Ruby's Tea Room
Lexington, North Carolina

Cashew Salad

2 C. precooked chicken strips

1 C. chopped celery

1 C. pineapple chunks,
  drained

½ C. firm grapes

½ C. water chestnuts, drained

¾ C. mayonnaise

1 tsp. soy sauce

1 T. curry powder

Cashew nuts for garnish

In a large metal mixing bowl, combine chicken strips, chopped celery, pineapple chunks, grapes and water chestnuts. To make dressing, in a blender, combine mayonnaise, soy sauce and curry powder. Pour dressing over ingredients in bowl and toss until evenly coated. Before serving, garnish with cashew nuts sprinkled over salad.

Elizabeth and Alexander's English Tea Room
Bothell, Washington

Lunchtime Salad

2 T. lemon juice
1 medium pear, cored
  and chopped
¾ C. cucumber, chopped
2 medium carrots, grated
½ C. shredded white cabbage
¾ C. (6 oz.) cubed Red
  Leicester cheese

3 oz. plain yogurt
2 T. whipped salad dressing
½ tsp. dried mixed herbs
2 tomatoes, cut into wedges
Whole wheat bread rolls

In a shallow bowl, place lemon juice. Dip chopped pears in lemon juice. In a large serving bowl, combine chopped pears, chopped cucumber, grated carrots, shredded cabbage and cubed Red Leicester cheese. In a medium bowl, combine plain yogurt, salad dressing and mixed herbs. Pour yogurt mixture over pear mixture and toss until evenly coated. Place tomato wedges around outside of bowl. Serve salad with whole wheat bread rolls.

The Front Parlour Tearoom at The British Shoppe
Madison, Connecticut

Chado's Punjab Wheels Sandwich

Makes 4 to 6 servings

3 tsp. Lapsang Souchong tea	2 tsp. finely chopped chives
8 hard-boiled eggs	Pinch of salt, optional
3 T. mayonnaise	8 slices bread, any kind

Prepare Lapsang Souchong tea, brewing for at least 10 minutes, until tea is strong. Peel hard-boiled eggs and place in a large bowl. Pour tea over eggs in bowl. Cover bowl and place in refrigerator and let eggs marinate for 36 hours. Remove eggs to a separate bowl and mash coarsely with a spatula. Add mayonnaise and chopped chives, mixing until evenly incorporated. If desired, mix in salt. Spread 2 tablespoons egg mixture onto each of the 4 slices of bread. Cover with remaining 4 slices of bread. Cut each sandwich into 4 triangles.

***Chado Tearoom,
Pasadena, California***

Panini Waffled Sandwich

Makes 2 sandwiches

2 T. butter, softened
4 slices marbled rye bread
2 T. grated Parmesan cheese

2 slices cooked ham or turkey
2 slices Swiss or Cheddar cheese

Generously spread butter onto 1 side of each slice of bread. Sprinkle grated Parmesan cheese over buttered sides of bread. Place 1 slice meat and 1 slice cheese on 2 slices of bread and top with remaining 2 slices of bread, buttered sides out. Grill sandwiches in a sandwich maker or lightly oiled frying pan for 5 to 8 minutes. The Parmesan cheese should make a crusty coating on the bread. Cut each sandwich in half and serve warm.

The Main Street Mill Historic Tea Room
Smithville, Missouri

Mango-Tango Chicken Salad

Makes 5 servings

3¼ C. cooked chopped chicken breasts

½ C. peeled and diced mango

½ C. diced fresh pineapple

½ C. sliced water chestnuts, drained

½ C. diced celery

¼ C. diced green onions

1 T. mango chutney

1 T. mayonnaise

1 T. sour cream

2 tsp. lemon juice

½ tsp. salt

1 tsp. peeled and minced fresh gingerroot

¼ tsp. pepper

10 slices peeled papaya

In a large bowl, combine chopped chicken, diced mango, diced pineapple, sliced water chestnuts, diced celery and diced green onions. In a small bowl, combine mango chutney, mayonnaise, sour cream, lemon juice, salt, minced gingerroot and pepper. Stir chutney mixture into chicken mixture. Arrange papaya slices around each plate. Prepare a small bed of lettuce and top with chicken salad.

Tale of Two Sisters Tearoom & Gift Shoppe
Red Wing, Minnesota

Date and Walnut Tea Sandwiches

½ C. pitted dates
⅓ C. walnut pieces
2 oz. cream cheese, softened

1 T. honey
¼ tsp. cinnamon
4 large slices fruit bread

In a blender or food processor, combine dates, walnuts, cream cheese, honey and cinnamon until the dates are finely chopped. Spread mixture over 1 side of 2 of the slices of fruit bread. Top each slice with a remaining slice of bread. Lightly press each sandwich together. Trim crusts and cut each sandwich into 4 triangles.

Miss Mable's Tea Room
Dickson, Tennessee

Lapsang Souchong Smoked Chicken Breast Sandwich with Herbed Goat Cheese and Apples

6 T. Lapsang Souchong tea

1 C. soy sauce

¾ C. balsamic vinegar

5 cloves garlic, chopped, divided

1 T. finely chopped fresh gingerroot

½ C. brown sugar

1 orange, halved and juiced

1 lemon, halved and juiced

Salt and pepper to taste

2 lbs. boneless chicken breast

6 oz. goat cheese

1 C. assorted chopped herbs (tarragon, chervil, thyme and/or chives)

¼ C. whole milk

Chinese 5 spice

7-grain bread, or any kind

Granny Smith apple slices

Brew tea in 12 ounces hot water. When tea is finished steeping, add ice to make about 14 ounces. In a large bowl, combine tea, soy sauce, balsamic vinegar, 4 cloves chopped garlic, chopped gingerroot, brown sugar, orange juice, lemon juice, salt and pepper. Place chicken in bowl and marinate for a minimum of 4 hours. Preheat oven to 450°. In a medium bowl, combine goat cheese, remaining 1 clove chopped garlic and assorted chopped herbs. Stir continuously while adding whole milk, until mixture is soft. Add salt and pepper. Smoke chicken in either a perforated pan or a fish poacher. On the bottom of pan, spread a small handful of brewed tea leaves. Place chicken in pan and sprinkle with salt, pepper and Chinese 5 spice on both sides. Cook chicken in oven for 25 to 30 minutes until internal temperature is 170°. The tea should dry out and smoke the chicken while cooking. Chill chicken in refrigerator. To prepare sandwich, spread a generous amount of goat cheese mixture on both sides of bread. Place thin apple slices on sandwich. Slice cooled chicken breast very thin and pile on top of apples.

Alice's Tea Cup
New York City, New York

Tandoori Chicken Wrap

2 T. soy sauce
1 tsp. cumin
1 tsp. ground turmeric
½ tsp. coriander
¼ tsp. ground red pepper
¼ tsp. grated orange peel
1 lb. chicken breast halves, de-boned and cut into strips
2 tsp. sesame oil or vegetable oil, divided
1½ C. julienne-cut carrots

8 (1″) green onions, sliced
¼ C. fresh chopped cilantro
1 C. plain yogurt
½ C. tomato sauce
¾ tsp. curry powder
¼ tsp. sugar
⅛ tsp. pepper
4 (6″) tortillas
¼ C. mango chutney, optional

In a medium bowl, combine soy sauce, cumin, turmeric, coriander, red pepper, grated orange peel and chicken strips. Stir to evenly coat chicken. Cover mixture and marinate in refrigerator for 30 minutes. In a large non-stick skillet over medium heat, heat 1 teaspoon oil. Add marinated chicken. Cook until chicken is done, about 8 minutes. Remove chicken from skillet and keep warm. Add remaining 1 teaspoon oil to skillet over medium high heat. Add carrots and green onions. Sauté for 10 minutes, until browned. Stir in chopped cilantro. To make sauce, in a large bowl, combine yogurt, tomato sauce, curry powder, sugar and pepper. Spread 3 tablespoons sauce over each tortilla. Top each with 1 cup chicken strips and ⅓ cup carrot mixture. Roll up tortillas. If desired, serve wraps with mango chutney.

Tale of Two Sisters Tearoom & Gift Shoppe
Red Wing, Minnesota

Indian Shrimp Sandwich

⅔ C. frozen medium shrimp	¼ tsp. curry powder
1 leaf red or green lettuce	1 honey stick
2 slices white or wheat bread	2 T. minced celery
2 T. mayonnaise	2 thin slices cucumber

Thaw shrimp by running under cool water for a few minutes. Drain shrimp and cut each piece into thirds. Rinse lettuce leaf and trim crusts from bread. In a medium stainless steel bowl, combine mayonnaise, curry powder and honey stick. Mix in shrimp and minced celery. Spread mixture over 1 slice of bread, add lettuce leaf, thin cucumber slices and top with other slice of bread. Cut sandwich in half diagonally. If desired, serve with fresh fruit and a cup of tea.

Retro Tea Room
Bowie, Maryland

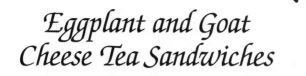

Eggplant and Goat Cheese Tea Sandwiches

1 eggplant, thinly sliced
1 large red pepper,
  thinly sliced
1 T. olive oil
Pinch of salt

2 T. butter, softened
1 clove garlic, minced
4 slices white or wheat bread
4 to 5 T. goat cheese

In a medium skillet over medium heat, sauté eggplant and red pepper slices in olive oil, until golden brown. Place eggplant and red peppers on a paper towel and sprinkle with salt. In a small bowl, cream together butter and minced garlic until well blended. Spread an even amount of butter and garlic mixture over each slice of bread. Place thin slices of eggplant and red pepper on each slice of bread. Top each slice with an even amount of goat cheese. Place slices in broiler and heat until golden brown. Trim crusts and cut into 4 triangles.

Miss Mable's Tea Room
Dickson, Tennessee

Grilled Shrimp

¼ C. olive oil
¼ C. fresh minced herbs
3 T. lemon juice
3 cloves garlic, crushed

1 T. minced shallots
Salt and pepper
1½ lbs. large shrimp,
  shelled and deveined

In a large bowl, combine olive oil, minced herbs, lemon juice, crushed garlic, minced shallots, salt and pepper. Marinate shrimp in mixture for 5 hours. Place marinated shrimp on skewers and cook over a hot grill. If desired, serve with Mango Salsa (page 14).

The Great Galena Peddlery
Galena, Illinois

Sweet & Sour Meatballs

1 lb. ground beef
½ C. dried bread crumbs
⅓ C. diced onion
¼ C. milk
1 egg
1 tsp. salt
1 T. Worcestershire sauce

½ tsp. pepper
2 T. vegetable oil
2 C. French dressing
½ C. apricot preserves
2 T. dried Lipton onion soup mix

Preheat oven to 325°. In a large bowl, combine ground beef, breadcrumbs, diced onions, milk, egg, salt, Worcestershire sauce, pepper and vegetable oil. Mix well and shape mixture into 2″ round balls. Bake for 25 to 30 minutes. In a separate bowl, combine French dressing, apricot preserves and onion soup mix. Pour mixture over meatballs and serve immediately.

A Spot For Tea
Oklahoma City, Oklahoma

Crab Soufflé

½ lb. flaked crabmeat
6 C. bread cubes
1 tsp. salt
1 small jar pimentos, drained
2 C. cooked noodles
2 T. chopped onion
  (or 2 tsp. dried onion)

1½ C. shredded Cheddar
  cheese
2 C. milk
⅔ C. butter, melted
6 eggs, beaten
½ C. bread crumbs

Preheat oven to 350°. In a large bowl, combine flaked crabmeat, bread cubes, salt, drained pimentos, cooked noodles, onions and shredded Cheddar cheese. In a separate bowl, scald milk over medium high heat. Pour hot milk and melted butter over crab mixture. Fold in beaten eggs. Pour mixture into a lightly greased soufflé dish or 9 x 13″ baking dish. Top with bread crumbs. Cover and bake for 45 minutes, removing cover for last 15 minutes of baking time.

The Rose Cottage Gift Shop & Tea Room
Clear Lake, Iowa

Mexican Egg Casserole

6 to 8 slices French bread,
    cut ¼″ thick

2 C. shredded Cheddar
    cheese

2 C. shredded Monterey
    Pepper Jack cheese

1 (7 oz.) can Ortega green
    chilies, diced

1 lb. crumbled cooked bacon
    or pork sausage

8 eggs

2 C. milk

2 tsp. salt

½ tsp. pepper

¼ tsp. dry mustard

Pinch of dried oregano

¼ tsp. garlic powder

Butter the French bread slices and place, buttered-side down, in a 9 x 13″ baking dish. Sprinkle shredded Cheddar and Monterey Pepper Jack cheeses over bread slices. Sprinkle diced chilies over cheese and spread crumbled cooked meat over chilies. In a large bowl, beat together eggs, milk, salt, pepper, dry mustard, dried oregano and garlic powder. Pour mixture over ingredients in pan. Cover and refrigerate overnight. Preheat oven to 325°. Bake for 50 minutes.

Rose Mountain Manor B&B and Tea Room
Colfax, California

Highland Beef Casserole

5 lbs. stew meat
  or ground sirloin
6 C. water
3 T. au jus
2 large onions, chopped
  (or 1 C. dried onion)
1 T. steak seasoning
½ C. whiskey

2 T. Worcestershire sauce
2 large leeks, sliced
7 carrots, peeled and
  chopped
6 large potatoes, peeled
  and diced
Beef gravy powder to thicken
2 C. frozen peas

In a large pot over medium heat, brown stew meat. Once meat has browned, add water. Add au jus, chopped onions, steak seasoning, whiskey and Worcestershire sauce. Let simmer until meat is tender. Add sliced leeks, chopped carrots and diced potatoes and cook until vegetables are tender. Thicken beef with gravy powder. Stir in frozen peas 5 minutes before serving. Spoon into bowls. If desired, serve over noodles.

Lady Caroline's British Tea Shop
Omaha, Nebraska

Vegetarian Lasagna

1 (14½ oz.) can diced
   tomatoes, drained

1 (15 oz.) can tomato sauce

1 C. chopped celery

1 C. chopped onion

1 C. chopped green bell
   pepper

1½ tsp. dried basil

1 egg, beaten

2 C. ricotta cheese
   or cottage cheese

¼ C. grated Parmesan cheese

1 (16 oz.) pkg. frozen
   chopped broccoli, cooked
   and drained

12 lasagna noodles, cooked
   and drained

1 C. shredded mozzarella
   cheese

Preheat oven to 350°. To make sauce, in a large saucepan over medium heat, combine drained tomatoes, tomato sauce, chopped celery, chopped onions, chopped green peppers and dried basil. Cook for 20 minutes, stirring occasionally. In a medium bowl, combine beaten egg, ricotta cheese, grated Parmesan cheese and cooked broccoli. Place ½ cup of the heated sauce in the bottom of a greased 9 x 13″ baking dish. Top sauce in dish with 4 cooked lasagna noodles. Place half of the cheese and broccoli mixture over noodles followed by half of the remaining sauce. Cover with 4 more cooked noodles, remaining half of the cheese and broccoli mixture and remaining half of the sauce. Top sauce with remaining 4 cooked noodles. Cover lasagna with shredded mozzarella cheese. Cover and bake for 30 minutes. Remove cover and bake an additional 5 minutes. Let stand for 10 minutes before serving.

A Perfect Blend
Lititz, Pennsylvania

Wild Rice Soup

½ C. uncooked wild rice
1 lb. bacon
3 T. bacon drippings
¾ C. chopped celery
1 C. chopped onion
½ C. chopped green pepper

2 (14½ oz.) cans chicken broth
1 (4 oz.) can sliced mushrooms, drained
8 oz. fresh mushrooms, sliced
3 (10½ oz.) cans cream of mushroom soup

Thoroughly wash wild rice. In a small pot, boil rice for 15 minutes. Drain and set aside. In a large skillet, fry bacon until crisp. Remove bacon and dice. Discard all but 3 tablespoons of bacon drippings. If the bacon drippings are not removed, the soup becomes extremely salty. Sauté chopped celery, chopped onions and chopped green pepper in drippings until onion are transparent. Transfer to a large soup pot and add cooked rice, diced bacon, chicken broth, canned and fresh mushrooms and cream of mushroom soup. Cook over low heat for 1 hour, being careful not to boil.

Tale of Two Sisters Tearoom & Gift Shoppe
Red Wing, Minnesota

Cream of Mushroom Soup with Sherry

2 large cans cream
of mushroom soup
1 large can milk
1 large can water

¾ C. sherry cooking wine
4 T. butter or margarine
Salt and pepper

In a crock pot, combine cream of mushroom soup, milk and water. Stir in sherry and butter. Add salt and pepper to taste. With crock pot on high setting, let soup warm for 1 to 1½ hours.

Tea Tyme & What Nots
Fredericksburg, Virginia

Tomato Basil Soup

6 C. water

1 large can chopped tomatoes with juice

1 large can tomato sauce

½ C. dried onion

1 T. au jus

2 T. dried or fresh chopped basil

2 T. sugar

In a large soup pot, place water. Add chopped tomatoes with juice and tomato sauce to pot. Stir in dried onion, au jus and basil. Bring to a boil over medium high heat. Reduce heat to low-medium and let simmer for 20 minutes. Stir in sugar. Serve hot. If desired, use soup as a base for minestrone or chill and use as a base for gazpacho.

Lady Caroline's British Tea Shop
Omaha, Nebraska

Victorian Soup

Makes 12 servings

2 T. butter
½ cucumber, peeled, seeded and chopped
1 C. fresh chopped mushrooms
1 onion, chopped
⅓ C. cooked chopped chicken
2 T. cooked ground ham

1 (10½ oz.) can asparagus, drained
1 T. cornstarch
2 T. water
4 C. chicken broth
2 egg yolks
½ C. heavy cream
Salt and pepper to taste

In a large saucepan, melt butter and sauté cucumber, mushrooms and onion for 10 minutes, being careful not to brown vegetables. Add chopped chicken, ground ham and drained asparagus. Sauté for an additional 5 minutes. Remove from heat and puree sautéed mixture in blender or food processor and return to saucepan. In a medium bowl, mix cornstarch with water. Add chicken broth. Pour liquid mixture into same saucepan and mix all together. Cook for 30 minutes over low heat. In a small bowl, combine egg yolks and heavy cream. Pour egg yolk mixture gradually into same saucepan and cook, being careful not to boil. Season with salt and pepper.

The Glenwood Village & Tearoom
Shreveport, Louisiana

Carrot & Cauliflower Soup

Makes 4 servings

1⅛ C. cubed carrots
⅞ C. cubed potatoes
½ C. cubed cauliflower
10 C. water, divided
½ tomato, finely chopped
½ tsp. salt

⅛ tsp. pepper
1 tsp. sesame oil
½ tsp. blended ginger paste
¼ C. fresh finely chopped cilantro

In a large soup pot, bring carrots, potatoes and cauliflower to a boil in 5 cups water. Boil for 10 minutes, drain and transfer to a blender or food processor. Puree vegetables and 3 cups water and return to soup pot. Add remaining 2 cups water. Boil mixture over medium heat for 20 minutes. Add finely chopped tomato, salt, pepper, sesame oil and blended ginger paste. Boil for an additional 2 minutes. Spoon soup into serving bowls and garnish with finely chopped cilantro.

Franchia Tea
New York City, New York

Creamy Asparagus Soup

2 large onions, chopped
4 T. margarine
4 T. flour
8 C. chicken broth
3 lbs. asparagus,
   cut into 1″ pieces

1 tsp. salt
½ tsp. white pepper
2 large potatoes, cut into
   1″ cubes
2 C. evaporated skim milk
Croutons, optional

In a large soup pot over medium heat, sauté onions in margarine for 5 minutes. Cook until onions are tender and transparent, but not browned. Add flour, stirring until mixture is bubbly. Whisk in chicken broth until flour has dissolved. Add asparagus, salt, white pepper and potatoes to soup pot. Bring mixture to a boil. Reduce heat, cover and let simmer for 20 minutes, until asparagus and potatoes are tender. Allow to cool for 10 minutes. Pour mixture into a blender or food processor and puree until smooth. Using a large strainer, strain soup, removing asparagus fibers, and return to soup pot. Add evaporated milk and cook over low heat until hot, but not boiling. Place soup in bowls. If desired, garnish with croutons. Soup freezes well in airtight containers. To reheat, microwave for 7 minutes, stirring after every 3 minutes, until hot.

Elise's Tea Room
Long Beach, California

Lobster Bisque

Makes 6 servings

1 (¾ to 1 lb.) lobster tail	1 tsp. dried tarragon
4 C. water	½ tsp. dried thyme
6 T. butter, divided	Pinch of red pepper flakes
⅓ C. brandy	2 bay leaves
½ C. finely minced shallots	3 T. flour
2 cloves garlic, minced	2½ C. whole milk
3 T. tomato paste	¾ C. heavy cream
2½ C. dry white wine	Salt and pepper

In a large pot, simmer lobster tail in water until just cooked. Remove lobster tail, reserving the water. Remove lobster meat from shell. Chop shell into 1″ pieces. Dice lobster meat and chill in refrigerator while preparing soup. In a large sauté pan over medium heat, melt 3 tablespoons butter. Add lobster shell pieces and brandy. Cook until brandy is almost evaporated. Add minced shallots and minced garlic and sauté until softened. Add tomato paste, white wine, tarragon, thyme, red pepper flakes, bay leaves and reserved cooking water. Simmer, uncovered, for 30 minutes. Strain mixture through a sieve into a large bowl. In a separate sauté pan, melt remaining 3 tablespoons butter. Stir in flour and cook, whisking constantly, for 1 minute. Add milk and heavy cream and cook until liquid is thickened. Add strained lobster broth and heat. Add diced lobster meat and heat throughout. Add salt and pepper to taste.

The Great Galena Peddlery
Galena, Illinois

Stilton & Fresh Pear Savoury Tart

30 (5″) pastry tart shells
3 lbs. Stilton blue cheese, crumbled

3 fresh pears
12 eggs
8 C. half n' half

Preheat oven to 375°. Place tart shells on lightly greased baking sheets. Crumble blue cheese and divide equally into tart shells. Core and slice pears and place pear slices on top of crumbled blue cheese. In a large bowl, beat together eggs and half n' half. Pour mixture over tarts. Bake for 30 to 40 minutes.

The Front Parlour Tearoom at The British Shoppe
Madison, Connecticut

73

Peanut Soup

Makes 18 to 20 servings

3 qts. chicken broth
4 stalks celery, chopped
2 medium onions, chopped
½ C. butter
¼ C. flour

2 C. creamy peanut butter
4 C. light cream
Chopped peanuts and fresh
   parsley sprigs, optional

In a large soup pot over medium heat, heat chicken broth, chopped celery and chopped onions, until vegetables are softened. Transfer broth and vegetables to a blender or food processor and puree until smooth. In a medium saucepan over medium heat, make a rue from butter and flour by melting butter and adding flour, little by little, until mixture is the consistency of gravy. Gradually mix in chicken broth puree. Add creamy peanut butter and whisk to blend. Stir in light cream. Serve soup by ladling into bowls. If desired, garnish with chopped peanuts and fresh parsley sprigs.

Jefferson Hill Tea Room
Naperville, Illinois

Cheese Soup

Makes 6 to 8 servings

¾ C. finely chopped carrots
½ C. finely chopped celery
¼ C. finely chopped onion
½ C. butter
1 C. Bisquick baking mix
½ tsp. paprika
⅛ tsp. pepper

⅛ tsp. ground red pepper
3 (10¾ oz.) cans chicken broth
2 C. half n' half
2 C. shredded sharp Cheddar cheese

In a large saucepan or pot over low-medium heat, cook chopped carrots, chopped celery and chopped onion in butter. Stir in Bisquick, paprika, pepper and red pepper. Remove from heat and gradually stir in chicken broth. Increase heat to medium, stirring constantly, until boiling. Boil and stir for 1 minute. Reduce heat and stir in half n' half and shredded sharp Cheddar cheese. Heat until cheese is melted.

The Rose Cottage Gift Shop & Tea Room
Clear Lake, Iowa

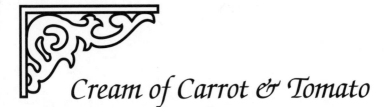

Cream of Carrot & Tomato

1 medium onion, diced	4 C. canned diced tomatoes, drained
6 T. butter, divided	1 C. heavy cream
2 lbs. carrots, peeled and diced	2 C. whole milk
1 (14½ oz.) can chicken broth	2 tsp. dried dillweed
4 T. flour	Sour cream for garnish

In a large saucepan over medium heat, sauté diced onions in 2 tablespoons butter. Add diced carrots and chicken broth, cooking until carrots are softened. Place heated mixture in a blender or food processor and puree. In a large pot over low heat, melt remaining 4 tablespoons butter. Stir in flour and pureed mixture, cooking until thickened. Add diced tomatoes, heavy cream, whole milk and dried dillweed. Cook until soup is heated throughout, being careful not to boil. To serve, ladle soup into bowls and garnish with a dollop of sour cream.

A Perfect Blend
Lititz, Pennsylvania

Desserts

Rich Chocolate Raspberry Truffles

Makes 4 dozen

1 (8 oz.) pkg. semi-sweet
   baking chocolate, melted
2½ C. crushed chocolate
   wafers
1 C. ground almonds

¾ C. powdered sugar
½ C. raspberry preserves
⅓ C. coffee-flavored liqueur
4 oz. white chocolate, melted

In a double boiler or saucepan, melt baking chocolate according to package directions. In a medium bowl, combine crushed chocolate wafers, ground almonds and powdered sugar. Mix well and blend in melted semi-sweet chocolate, raspberry preserves and coffee liqueur. Shape mixture into 1″ balls. Place balls on a baking sheet and refrigerate for 15 minutes. Top each ball with a dollop of melted white chocolate.

Tranquili-tea Tea Room
Denver, Colorado

MacNab's Famous Lemon Curd

1 C. butter
1½ C. sugar

Juice and zest of 4 lemons, divided
4 eggs

In a double boiler over medium heat, melt together butter, sugar, half of the lemon juice and half of the lemon zest. In a medium bowl, whisk together eggs, remaining half of the lemon juice and remaining half of the lemon zest. When butter mixture is completely melted, whisk in egg mixture. Whisk rapidly, until lemon curd thickens, curdling when dropped from the whisk. Transfer to an airtight container and chill in refrigerator until ready to serve.

MacNab's Tea Room
Boothbay, Maine

Quick and Easy
Tiny Tart Shells

1 lb. butter, softened   **1 C. powdered sugar**
1 tsp. vanilla   **4½ to 5 C. flour**

Preheat oven to 375°. Lightly grease the cups of mini muffin tins. In a large mixing bowl, beat together butter, vanilla and powdered sugar at medium-high speed. Slowly add flour until dough reaches the consistency of clay. Shape dough into small balls. Place 1 ball into each muffin cup. Press dough on bottom and up sides of each muffin cup to shape the tart shells. Bake for about 8 minutes. Cool and fill with Strawberry Fluff Tart Filling (page 88) or any other tart filling.

the shoppe at Shady Gables
Authentic English Tearoom and Gift Gallery
Versailles, Missouri

Easy Apple Dumplings

2 large apples
1 can (6 to 8 rolls)
  crescent rolls
¾ C. sugar

1 C. orange juice
6 T. butter
Cinnamon

Preheat oven to 350°. Peel, core and quarter apples. Halve apples for large dumplings. Separate crescent rolls. Spread an even amount of apples over each crescent roll. Wrap crescent rolls to secure apples. In a medium saucepan, melt sugar, orange juice and butter. Place wrapped apples in baking dish and pour melted mixture over apples. Sprinkle with cinnamon. Bake for 20 to 30 minutes, until golden brown.

Tale of Two Sisters Tearoom & Gift Shoppe
Red Wing, Minnesota

Chocolate Tiramisu Crepes

Makes 8 servings

2 eggs
1 C. milk
½ C. flour
2 T. cocoa powder
1 C. plus 1 T. sugar, divided
¼ tsp. salt

3 T. butter, melted
8 oz. cream cheese, softened
1 tsp. vanilla
2 T. instant espresso powder
1 C. heavy whipping cream
Cocoa powder for garnish

In a medium bowl, whisk together eggs and milk. Add flour, cocoa powder, 1 tablespoon sugar, salt and melted butter. Mix well with a whisk or in blender. Let sit for 30 minutes. Heat a large pan over medium-high heat. Use ¼ cup batter for each crepe. Drop batter into hot pan and swirl pan to cover bottom. Bake until crepe starts to dry at the edges. Flip crepe to cook other side. To make filling, in a medium bowl, combine cream cheese and remaining 1 cup sugar until thoroughly combined. Add vanilla and espresso powder. Mix until espresso is evenly distributed. In a separate bowl, whip heavy cream until stiff peaks form. Fold whipped cream into espresso mixture. Serve crepes warm with filling spread over top. If desired, garnish with a sprinkle of cocoa powder. Both crepe batter and filling can be made ahead of time and assembled just before serving.

The Great Galena Peddlery
Galena, Illinois

Chocolate Rum Raspberry Torte

1 lb. butter, softened, divided
1⅔ C. Hershey's cocoa, divided
4 C. sugar
6 eggs
4 T. rum

2 C. flour
Raspberry filling
2 C. powdered sugar
5 T. half n' half

Preheat oven to 350°. In a microwave-safe dish, melt 1½ cups butter in microwave for 90 seconds. In a large mixing bowl, combine melted butter and 1 cup cocoa at low speed. Add sugar and eggs and mix well. Blend in rum and flour. Gradually increase mixer to high speed, blending until mixture is creamy and smooth. Grease 4 round cake or torte pans with a false bottom. Pour ¼ of the mixture into each cake pan. Bake for 15 minutes. Rotate cakes from front of oven to back or vice versa. Bake an additional 5 minutes. Remove pans from oven and let cool. Once cakes have cooled, place one cake on a cake stand or serving platter. Spread raspberry filling across top of cake. Layer with another cake and raspberry filling. Repeat until all cakes have been layered. Do not put raspberry filling on top of the fourth cake. In a medium bowl, combine remaining ½ cup butter, remaining ⅔ cup cocoa, powdered sugar and half n' half. Mix well to create frosting. Frost the top and sides of cake.

Elizabeth and Alexander's English Tea Room
Bothell, Washington

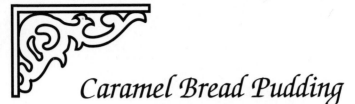

Caramel Bread Pudding

Makes 6 servings

1 C. brown sugar	3 C. milk
3 slices bread, cut into cubes	1 tsp. vanilla
3 eggs, beaten	Salt to taste

Preheat oven to 350°. In the bottom of a greased 9 x 13″ baking dish, sprinkle brown sugar evenly. Layer bread cubes over brown sugar. In a medium bowl, combine beaten eggs, milk, vanilla and salt. Mix well and pour over bread cubes in baking dish. Do not stir. Fill a large roasting pan with hot water and set baking dish inside roasting pan. Place both pans in oven and bake for 40 minutes.

The Wenham Tea House and Shops
Wenham, Massachusetts

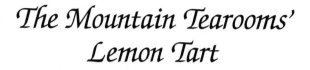

The Mountain Tearooms' Lemon Tart

Zest of 3 lemons
6 egg yolks
3 eggs
1½ C. sugar

1 C. heavy cream
Juice of 5 lemons
1 (10″) baked pie crust

In a large mixing bowl, combine lemon zest, egg yolks and eggs. Beat, using the paddle or beating attachment, for 10 seconds. Add sugar and beat at high speed until mixture has tripled in volume, about 5 minutes. Meanwhile, prepare a pan of boiling water large enough to hold the large mixing bowl. Keep the water at a rolling boil. Add heavy cream to egg mixture. Beat at low speed until well combined. Set mixing bowl over pan of boiling water. Add lemon juice to mixing bowl and stir, using a spatula, until the mixture has thickened, about 10 to 15 minutes. Remove mixing bowl from pan of water. Run mixture through a strainer into the baked pie crust. Mixture should resemble barely set Jell-O. If tart is too runny, place in a 200° oven for 10 minutes, being careful not to overcook, as mixture will separate. Let lemon tart cool and refrigerate. Serve at room temperature.

The Mountain Tearooms
Long Valley, New Jersey

Strawberry & Chocolate Trifle

Makes 8 servings

1½ lbs. strawberries	½ C. brown sugar
4 T. orange juice	3 eggs, separated
2 T. orange liqueur, such as Cointreau or Grand Marnier, optional	8 chocolate brownies
	Frozen whipped topping, thawed
1 lb. plus ¼ C. mascarpone cheese	¼ C. dark chocolate, grated or curled

Wash, hull and slice the strawberries. In a large bowl, combine strawberries, orange juice and orange liqueur. Set aside for 30 minutes. In a separate bowl, beat together mascarpone, brown sugar and egg yolks until smooth. In a separate bowl, whip egg whites until soft peaks form. Fold egg whites into mascarpone mixture. Break brownies into small pieces. Layer half of the broken brownies evenly into 8 dessert glasses. Layer half of the strawberry mixture over brownies in glasses. Layer half of the mascarpone mixture over strawberries in glasses. Top with another layer of remaining brownies followed by another layer of remaining strawberries. Top glasses with remaining mascarpone mixture. Cover glasses with plastic wrap and chill in refrigerator until ready to serve. Before serving, top glasses with a dollop of whipped topping and grated or curled chocolate.

Note: The US FDA does not recommend eating raw eggs.

Brewster Teapot at the Beechcroft Inn
Brewster, Massachusetts

Our Famous Chocolate Fanfare Tart

Makes 12 servings

1¾ C. flour, divided

2 T. brown sugar

4½ C. chocolate chips, divided

6 T. cold butter, diced

2 to 3 T. milk

4 tsp. vanilla, divided

½ C. butter, melted and boiling

1½ C. sugar

3 eggs

1 T. grated orange peel

1 C. heavy cream

Preheat oven to 350°. To make crust, in a blender or food processor, combine 1 cup flour, brown sugar and 1 cup chocolate chips. Process until chocolate chips are finely ground. Add 6 tablespoons diced cold butter and process until mixture is crumbly. Add milk and 1 teaspoon vanilla and mix until dough is workable. Press dough into a greased 11″ springform tart pan. Bake until crust is set. To make filling, in a medium bowl, combine 1½ cups chocolate chips and ½ cup boiling butter. Stir until well combined and smooth. In a separate bowl, combine sugar, eggs and remaining 3 teaspoons vanilla. Stir in melted chocolate and butter mixture. Add remaining ¾ cup flour and grated orange peel. Mix well and pour mixture into baked tart crust. Bake for about 35 minutes, until tart is almost cooked throughout, being careful not to over cook. To make topping, in a medium saucepan over medium heat, bring heavy cream to a boil. In a medium bowl, combine boiling heavy cream and remaining 2 cups chocolate chips and mix until smooth. Spread melted mixture over cooled tart. Refrigerate until ready to serve.

White Lilac Tearoom
Stratford, Connecticut

Strawberry Fluff Tart Filling

2 T. powdered sugar
1½ C. heavy whipping cream
3 C. angel food cake crumbs

1½ C. crushed strawberries
½ C. almonds, toasted*

In a medium bowl, combine powdered sugar and heavy cream. Beat mixture until stiff peaks form. Add angel food cake crumbs and crushed strawberries. Chill in refrigerator. Spoon mixture into cooled Tiny Tart Shells (page 80). Top with toasted almonds.

To toast, place almonds in a single layer on a baking sheet. Bake at 350° for approximately 10 minutes or until nuts are golden brown.

the shoppe at Shady Gables
Authentic English Tearoom and Gift Gallery
Versailles, Missouri

Miss Mable's Cookie Jar Tea Cakes

Makes 2 dozen tea cakes

⅔ C. shortening
¾ C. sugar
1 egg
½ tsp. vanilla

½ tsp. salt
2 C. flour
1½ tsp. baking powder
2 T. milk

Preheat oven to 375°. In a medium bowl, cream together shortening and sugar. Add egg and beat mixture until light and fluffy. Add vanilla. Sift together salt, flour, baking powder and add to cream mixture. Add milk and mix well. Divide dough in half and chill in refrigerator for 1 hour. Roll dough out to approximately ⅛" thickness. Cut into circles, or any shape, and pat onto a greased baking sheet. Bake for about 10 minutes, until lightly browned.

Miss Mable's Tea Room
Dickson, Tennessee

Shortbread

4 C. flour   **1 lb. butter**
1 C. sugar

Preheat oven to 325°. In a large bowl, combine flour and sugar. Cut in butter with a pastry blender until combined and mixture resembles cornmeal, being careful not to over mix. Pour mixture into a greased 9 x 13″ baking dish. Pat down mixture firmly by hand and prick with a fork. Bake for 30 to 40 minutes, until light golden brown. While still warm, cut and score shortbread into desired shapes. If shortbread cools before being cut and scored into shapes, it will crumble.

Tastefully British Shop and Tea Room
Sarasota, Florida

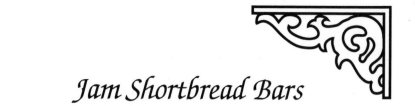

Jam Shortbread Bars

1 pkg. yellow cake mix	**4 T. butter, softened**
½ C. chopped pecans or	**1 egg**
favorite nuts	**8 oz. jam, any kind**

Preheat oven to 350°. Grease and flour a 9 x 13″ baking dish. Line pan with parchment paper. In a large mixing bowl, combine cake mix and chopped nuts. Mix at low speed for 2 minutes. Add butter, 1 tablespoon at a time, and mix until blended. In a small bowl, slightly beat egg and add to mixture. Beat at low speed until mixture begins to stick to sides of mixing bowl. Pour into prepared pan. Spread jam over mixture in pan. Bake for 20 to 25 minutes. If desired, drizzle a glaze over warm bars and cut into small diamond shapes.

Tale of Two Sisters Tearoom & Gift Shoppe
Red Wing, Minnesota

Oatmeal Cookies

Makes 50 to 60 cookies

1¼ C. flour
1 tsp. baking soda
1 C. butter, softened
¼ C. sugar
¾ C. brown sugar

1 (4 oz.) pkg. instant vanilla
  pudding mix
2 eggs
3½ C. old fashioned oats
1 C. raisins

Preheat oven to 375°. In a small bowl, combine flour and baking soda. In a large bowl, combine butter, sugar, brown sugar and vanilla pudding mix. Beat together until well blended. Add eggs to mixture. Gradually stir in flour mixture, oats and raisins. Drop dough by tablespoonfuls onto greased baking sheets. Bake for 10 to 12 minutes.

Aprille's Showers Tea Room
Farmington, Minnesota

Strawberry Bell Cookies

Makes 5 dozen

1 C. butter, softened	2 C. flour
3 oz. cream cheese, softened	¾ C. strawberry jam
¼ C. sugar	Powdered sugar
1 tsp. vanilla	

In a medium bowl, combine butter, cream cheese and sugar, until well blended. Mix in vanilla and gradually stir in flour. Cover bowl and chill in refrigerator for 15 minutes. Preheat oven to 375°. On a flat, lightly floured surface, roll half of the dough to ⅛″ thickness. Cut out cookies with a 2″ round cookie cutter. Repeat with remaining half of dough. Place cookies on lightly greased baking sheets. Place ½ teaspoon strawberry jam in the center of each circle. Fold up edges of dough to cover jam, leaving an opening at the top so some of the jam is still exposed. Bake for 8 to 10 minutes. Remove to wire racks to cool. If desired, dust cookies with powdered sugar before serving.

A Perfect Blend
Lititz, Pennsylvania

Tea Cakes

1 C. butter, softened	2 lbs. cake flour
2 C. powdered sugar	Additional powdered sugar
2 tsp. vanilla	2 T. milk
6 eggs	Colored sprinkles, optional

Preheat oven to 400°. In a medium mixing bowl, combine butter and powdered sugar at medium speed until creamy. Add vanilla and eggs, mixing until well blended. Gradually add cake flour, mixing with a wooden spoon until moist and well mixed. Divide dough into sections. Roll each section by hand into a rope. Tie a part of the rope into a knot and cut knot from rope. Be careful not to make knots too big, as cookies rise considerably while cooking. Repeat until all the dough has been used. Place cookie knots on a greased baking sheet. Bake for 10 to 13 minutes. Remove from oven and let cool. To make glaze, combine enough powdered sugar with milk, until glaze reaches desired spreading consistency. Brush glaze over cookies. If desired, decorate cookies with colored sprinkles.

Sheffield's Tea Room
Wallace, North Carolina

Mousse

Makes 4 large or 10 small mousse cups

1 T. instant espresso	3 egg whites
¾ C. chocolate pistoles, chunks or chips	¼ C. sugar
1 (13½ oz.) carton heavy whipping cream	

Dissolve instant espresso in a little hot water. Over a double boiler, melt the chocolate, stirring, until hot to the touch. In a medium bowl, combine dissolved espresso and heavy cream and whip to a very soft peak. Set aside. In a separate bowl, whip egg whites until white and creamy. Add sugar to egg whites and continue whipping to a soft peak. Thoroughly whip 1 scoop of the whipped cream and 1 scoop of the egg whites into the melted chocolate. In small, alternating batches, fold in remaining whipped cream and egg whites, until smooth and even. Transfer mousse to individual cups and chill in refrigerator for 1 hour.

Tips: Do not overheat chocolate or it will burn. However, if chocolate is not hot enough, it will seize and leave granules of chocolate in the mousse. Be careful not to over-whip the cream or egg whites or they will not mix well together. The mousse should seem somewhat soft when you are finished, but will set in the refrigerator.

Alice's Tea Cup
New York City, New York

Eggnog Mousse

Makes 4 to 5 servings

1 pkg. instant vanilla pudding mix	¼ to ½ tsp. nutmeg
2 C. cold eggnog	1 to 2 tsp. rum extract
	1 C. heavy whipping cream

In a medium bowl, whisk together pudding mix and cold eggnog for 2 minutes. Add nutmeg and rum extract. In a separate bowl, whip heavy cream to stiff peaks. Fold whipped cream into eggnog mixture. Refrigerate until set, about 1 hour. If desired, garnish with whipped cream and a sprinkle of nutmeg.

Chantilly Tea Room & Gift Boutique
Tucson, Arizona

Belle's Tea Cottage
Chocolate Cherry Cobbler

3 eggs, divided
1 (2 layer) pkg. chocolate
   cake mix
¾ C. butter, softened
4 C. powdered sugar, sifted

8 oz. cream cheese, softened
1 (21 oz.) can cherry pie
   filling
Heavy whipping cream,
   whipped

Preheat oven to 350°. In a large bowl, lightly beat 1 egg. Add chocolate cake mix and butter and beat until well blended. Press cake mixture into the bottom of a greased and floured 9 x 13" baking dish. In a medium bowl, combine sifted powdered sugar, cream cheese and remaining 2 eggs. Mix well and pour over cake mixture in pan. Spread cherry pie filling evenly over cream cheese layer. Bake for 30 to 40 minutes, until edges are lightly browned and center of cobbler is almost set. Let cool completely. Cover and chill in refrigerator until ready to serve. To serve, scoop cobbler into tea cups. Microwave until hot and garnish with 1 to 2 teaspoons whipped cream on top of each serving.

Belle's Tea Cottage
Reno, Nevada

Peach Cobbler

4 C. sliced fresh peaches
1½ C. sugar, divided
½ tsp. cinnamon
1 C. flour, sifted
1 tsp. baking powder

¼ tsp. salt
1 egg, well beaten
½ C. evaporated milk
½ C. butter, softened
½ tsp. almond extract

Preheat oven to 325°. Place fresh sliced peaches in the bottom of a greased 9″ square baking dish. In a small bowl, combine ½ cup sugar and cinnamon. Sprinkle mixture over peaches in pan. In a medium bowl, combine sifted flour, remaining 1 cup sugar, baking powder and salt. In a large bowl, beat together well beaten egg, evaporated milk, butter and almond extract. Add dry ingredients and blend until smooth. Pour mixture over peaches in pan. Bake for 1 hour, until cobbler is set. If desired, serve with vanilla ice cream.

Rose Mountain Manor B&B and Tea Room
Colfax, California

Grasshopper Pie

**17 chocolate sandwich
cookies, crushed**
¼ C. butter, melted
25 marshmallows

½ C. milk
3 T. crème de menthe
**1 C. heavy whipping cream,
whipped**

Set aside ¼ cup crushed cookies. In a medium bowl, combine remaining crushed cookies and melted butter. Press cookie and butter mixture into the bottom and up sides of a greased 9″ pie pan. In a double boiler, combine marshmallows and milk, heating until melted. Let cool slightly and stir in crème de menthe. Fold in whipped cream. Spread mixture into prepared pan. Sprinkle with reserved ¼ cup cookies. Chill in refrigerator for 2 hours before serving.

The Wenham Tea House and Shops
Wenham, Massachusetts

Cream Cheese Pecan Pie

2 (3 oz.) pkgs. cream cheese, softened
¼ C. plus 2 T. sugar, divided
4 eggs, divided
1 tsp. salt
2 tsp. vanilla, divided
¾ C. corn syrup
1 (9″) unbaked pie crust
1¼ C. chopped pecans

Preheat oven to 375°. In a small bowl, beat together cream cheese, ¼ cup sugar, 1 egg, salt and 1 teaspoon vanilla. Stir until mixture is thickened and creamy. In a separate bowl, beat remaining 3 eggs. Add corn syrup, remaining 2 tablespoons sugar and remaining 1 teaspoon vanilla. Beat until just blended. Spread cream cheese mixture evenly over the bottom of pie crust. Sprinkle chopped pecans over cream cheese layer. Gently pour corn syrup mixture over pecans in pie shell. Bake on lower rack of oven for 35 to 40 minutes.

Variation: To make miniature pecan pies, combine 1 (3 ounce) package cream cheese, ½ cup oleo, 1 cup flour and 1 tablespoon sugar. Mix until blended and form dough into small balls. Place 1 ball into each cup of mini muffin tins. Press crust into bottom and up sides of cups to form crusts. Fill with chopped pecans and corn syrup mixture from above. Bake in 350° oven for about 25 minutes.

Joie De Vie Tea Salon
Des Moines, Iowa

Banoffee Mess

Makes 6 servings

1 C. heavy whipping cream, whipped
6 large meringues
3 bananas, peeled and sliced

6 T. toffee or caramel sauce
6 T. chopped hazelnuts, toasted*

In a large bowl, place whipped cream. Crumble meringues over whipped cream. Carefully fold in sliced bananas. Swirl in toffee or caramel sauce. Spoon mixture evenly into 6 dessert glasses. Top with toasted hazelnuts and serve immediately.

* To toast, place chopped hazelnuts in a single layer on a baking sheet. Bake at 350° for approximately 10 minutes or until hazelnuts are golden brown.

Brewster Teapot at the Beechcroft Inn
Brewster, Massachusetts

Bakewell Slice

2 sheets flaky puff pastry	2 tsp. almond extract
Seedless raspberry jam	3 eggs, beaten
¾ C. butter, softened	2 C. self-rising flour, divided
1½ C. sugar	1 C. sliced almonds

Preheat oven to 375°. Line a baking sheet with puff pastry sheets. Spread raspberry jam over puff pastry. In a medium bowl, cream together butter and sugar, until light and fluffy. Blend in almond extract and beaten eggs, adding 1 tablespoon flour with the last egg. Fold in remaining flour, mixing with a metal spoon. Spread mixture evenly over raspberry jam layer. Bake for 25 minutes, until golden brown. Let cool and store in an airtight container. To serve, slice into bite size squares.

Lady Caroline's British Tea Shop
Omaha, Nebraska

MacKay Apricot Bars

1 C. dried apricots
½ C. butter, softened
¼ C. sugar
1⅓ C. flour, sifted, divided
½ tsp. baking powder
¼ tsp. salt

1 C. brown sugar
2 eggs, beaten
½ tsp. vanilla
½ C. coarsely chopped
  walnuts
Powdered sugar for dusting

Preheat oven to 350°. In a medium saucepan, place dried apricots. Cover apricots with water and bring to a boil. Let boil for 10 minutes and drain saucepan. Let apricots cool. Chop cooled apricots and set aside. In a medium bowl, combine butter, sugar and 1 cup sifted flour with a pastry blender. Mix until crumbly and press into a lightly greased 8″ square pan. Bake for 25 minutes, until lightly browned. Remove from oven and set aside. In a separate bowl, sift together remaining ⅓ cup flour, baking powder and salt. In a separate bowl, beat together brown sugar and eggs. Gradually stir flour and baking powder mixture into egg mixture. Add vanilla, chopped walnuts and chopped apricots. Mix well and spread over baked layer. Return to oven and bake for an additional 25 to 30 minutes. Remove from oven and let cool in pan before cutting into bars. Dust with powdered sugar.

MacNab's Tea Room
Boothbay, Maine

Aprille's Fairy Drops

Makes 50 to 60 servings

4½ C. flour	1 C. powdered sugar
1 tsp. baking soda	1 C. sugar
1 tsp. cream of tartar	1 C. vegetable oil
1 tsp. salt	2 eggs
1 C. butter, softened	2 tsp. almond extract

In a large bowl, combine flour, baking soda, cream of tartar and salt. In a separate bowl, beat butter until creamy. Stir in powdered sugar and sugar, beating until fluffy. Stir in vegetable oil, eggs and almond extract, until well blended. Stir in dry ingredients, mixing until just combined. Cover bowl and chill in refrigerator for 30 minutes. Preheat oven to 350°. Roll dough into 1″ balls and place on a greased baking sheet. Flatten dough with the back of a spoon to ¼″ thickness. Bake for 10 to 12 minutes, until edges are lightly browned. Let cool on a wire rack.

Almond Frosting

½ C. butter, softened	2 to 3 C. powdered sugar
½ tsp. almond extract	3 T. light cream
½ tsp. vanilla	Food coloring, optional

In a medium bowl, combine butter, almond extract, vanilla, powdered sugar and light cream. Beat well until mixture is creamy. If desired, mix in drops of food coloring. Spread frosting over cookies.

Aprille's Showers Tea Room
Farmington, Minnesota

Mom's Awesome Cheesecake

Makes 8 to 10 servings

2 (8 oz.) pkgs. cream cheese, softened

¾ C. sugar

2 T. fresh lemon juice

2 C. heavy cream, whipped to soft peaks

1 tsp. vanilla

2 pkgs. ladyfingers

2 pints fresh strawberries, hulled

½ C. currant jelly, melted

In a large mixing bowl, beat together cream cheese and sugar until smooth. Add lemon juice and whip until mixture is smooth and fluffy. Fold in whipped cream and vanilla. Line the bottom and sides of a 9″ springform pan with ladyfingers. Pour cream cheese mixture over ladyfingers in pan. Cover and refrigerate for at least 3 hours. Before serving, decorate top of cake with fresh strawberries. For a shiny topping, pour melted jelly over strawberries.

White Lilac Tearoom
Stratford, Connecticut

Turtle Cheesecake

2 C. vanilla wafer crumbs

½ C. butter, softened

1 (14 oz.) pkg. caramels, wrappers removed

1 can evaporated milk

2 C. chopped pecans, divided

4 (8 oz.) pkgs. cream cheese, softened

1 C. sugar

2 tsp. vanilla

4 eggs

½ C. chocolate chips

¼ C. heavy whipping cream

Preheat oven to 350°. In a large bowl, combine vanilla wafer crumbs and butter. Blend well and press into the bottom and up sides of a 10″ springform pan. Bake for 8 minutes, until set. Remove from oven and let cool. In a saucepan or double boiler over medium heat, melt caramels in evaporated milk, stirring until smooth. Let caramel mixture cool for 5 minutes and pour into cooled crust. Top caramel with 1½ cups chopped pecans. In a separate bowl, beat cream cheese until smooth. Add sugar and vanilla and mix well. Add eggs, one at a time, beating after each addition. Pour mixture into pan over caramels and pecans. Bake for 55 minutes, until filling is almost set. Let cool on wire rack and remove sides of pan. To make chocolate glaze, in a double boiler over medium heat, melt together chocolate chips and heavy cream. Stir until smooth and immediately spread over cheesecake. Sprinkle top of cake with remaining ½ cup chopped pecans.

The Rose Cottage Gift Shop & Tea Room
Clear Lake, Iowa

Lavender Pound Cake

2¼ C. flour
2 C. sugar
½ tsp. salt
½ tsp. baking soda
3 eggs

1 C. butter, softened
1 container lemon yogurt
2 tsp. natural dried lavender
Frosting, optional

Preheat oven to 325°. In a large mixing bowl, combine flour, sugar, salt, baking soda, eggs, butter, lemon yogurt and dried lavender at low speed until evenly blended. Increase speed to medium and beat for 3 minutes. Pour batter into a greased bundt pan. Bake for 60 to 70 minutes. Let cake cool on a wire rack before inverting cake onto serving plate. If desired, top cake with lemon juice and powdered sugar frosting.

Tastefully British Shop and Tea Room
Sarasota, Florida

Pumpkin Pie Cake

1 large can pumpkin puree
1 (13 oz.) can evaporated
 milk
3 eggs
1¼ C. sugar
1 tsp. allspice
¾ tsp. ground ginger

2 tsp. cinnamon
½ tsp. salt
1 box yellow cake mix
1 C. chopped nuts
¾ C. butter, melted
Whipped cream, optional

Preheat oven to 350°. In a large bowl, combine pumpkin puree, evaporated milk, eggs, sugar, allspice, ground ginger, cinnamon and salt. Mix well and pour into a greased 9 x 13″ baking dish. Sprinkle dry yellow cake mix over pumpkin mixture and gently pat down. Sprinkle chopped nuts over cake mix in pan. Drizzle melted butter over ingredients in pan. Bake for 50 minutes. Let cool before cutting into squares. If desired, serve with whipped cream.

Rose Mountain Manor B&B and Tea Room
Colfax, California

Vanilla Almond Raspberry Cake

1 box Betty Crocker golden vanilla cake mix
1 C. Crisco shortening
2¾ C. powdered sugar
1 tsp. almond extract

3 to 4 T. milk
1 small jar seedless raspberry jam
Frosting, optional

Bake cake according to box instructions, using two 8″ or 9″ round pans. Remove from oven and let cool. Meanwhile, in a large bowl, combine shortening, powdered sugar, almond extract and milk. Mix well and set aside. Place one cake onto serving plate and spread raspberry jam on top. Top with other cake. If desired, spread frosting over entire cake and serve.

Tea Tyme & What Nots
Fredericksburg, Virginia

Flourless Chocolate Cake

9 large eggs
1 lb. plus 4 T. unsalted
   butter, softened
1 C. cold strong-brewed
   coffee

1 lb. plus ¼ C. chopped
   semi-sweet chocolate
2¼ C. sugar
Whipped cream

Preheat oven to 250°. Lightly but thoroughly grease a sheet of aluminum foil large enough to line a 10″ springform pan. Line pan and set aside. In a medium bowl, whisk eggs and set aside. In a 3-quart saucepan over low heat, combine butter, cold coffee, chopped chocolate and sugar. Heat about 10 to 15 minutes, stirring constantly, until mixture reaches 130° and sugar dissolves, making sure not to overheat. Remove from heat and whisk in beaten eggs. Mix until thoroughly combined. Pour batter into prepared pan. Bake for 2 hours, until cake is set. Let cake cool completely on a wire rack. Cover cake loosely and chill in refrigerator. To serve, invert cake onto plate and carefully remove foil. Serve with whipped cream.

Note: Cake is best if allowed to "rest" a few days in refrigerator after baking.

Jefferson Hill Tea Room
Naperville, Illinois

Raspberry Chocolate Genoise

6 large eggs
2 egg yolks
1 C. sugar
2 C. flour, sifted
1 C. heavy whipping cream
1 C. chocolate chips

1 pkg. raspberry
   flavored gelatin
1 C. water
2 T. cornstarch
1 oz. Bacardi Razz or any
   raspberry flavored liqueur

Preheat oven to 350°. In a double boiler over medium heat, combine eggs, egg yolks and sugar, whisking frequently, until egg mixture is light in color, foamy and tripled in volume. Remove mixing bowl from heat and whip batter at medium high speed until stiff, about 7 to 10 minutes. Fold in sifted flour until fully incorporated, being careful not to overmix. Pour batter into a greased large 9 x 13″ baking dish. Bake for about 10 minutes, until lightly browned and springy to the touch. Set aside to cool. To prepare filling, in a double boiler, heat heavy cream until small bubbles start to form. Add chocolate chips and stir until fully incorporated. Remove mixture from heat and allow to cool to room temperature and thicken. To prepare sauce, in a medium saucepan, bring raspberry gelatin and water to a boil. Add cornstarch and continue to boil until thickened. Remove from heat and stir in raspberry liqueur. To assemble, cut cake into 2 equal halves. Spread half of the filling over 1 cake. Place second half on top and spread remaining filling over cake. Pour raspberry sauce over top of cake. Cut cake into squares and serve immediately. Can be refrigerated up to 1 week.

A Spot For Tea
Oklahoma City, Oklahoma

French Chocolate Cake

7 oz. bittersweet chocolate
1 C. butter
6 large eggs, separated
1 C. sugar

Powdered sugar for dusting
Crème fraiche and
   strawberries for garnish*

Preheat oven to 375°. Grease a 9″ springform pan and set aside. In a double boiler, melt chocolate and butter. Mix well and set aside to cool. In a medium bowl, beat egg whites until stiff. Gradually beat in sugar and egg yolks until mixture is creamy. Fold melted chocolate into egg mixture. Pour mixture into prepared pan. Bake for 55 minutes. The cake should puff up and sink when removed from the heat. Dust with powdered sugar. If desired, serve with crème fraiche and strawberries.

To make crème fraiche, whip together ½ cup heavy cream and 1 tablespoon sour cream. Let sit at room temperature until mixture thickens. Store in refrigerator up to 1 week.

The Great Galena Peddlery
Galena, Illinois

Carrot Cake

1½ C. vegetable oil
2 C. sugar
4 eggs
2 C. flour
1 tsp. baking powder
1 tsp. baking soda
1 tsp. cinnamon

¼ tsp. salt
2 C. grated carrots
1 (8 oz.) pkg. cream cheese, softened
½ C. butter, softened
2¾ C. powdered sugar
1 tsp. vanilla

Preheat oven to 350°. In a large mixing bowl, beat vegetable oil and sugar at low speed. Add eggs, one at a time. Slowly add flour, baking powder, baking soda, cinnamon and salt. Mix until well blended. Add grated carrots and mix at low speed until combined. Transfer to a greased 9 x 13" baking dish. Bake until a toothpick inserted in center of cake comes out clean. Meanwhile, in a large bowl, combine cream cheese, butter, powdered sugar and vanilla. Mix until smooth. Spread cream cheese mixture over cooled carrot cake.

Tea Tyme & What Nots

Miss Fannie's Pound Cake

1 C. butter, softened
2 C. sugar
5 eggs
2 C. flour, sifted

1 T. lemon juice
2 tsp. vanilla
1 tsp. almond extract

Preheat oven to 350°. In a medium mixing bowl, beat together butter and sugar at medium speed until creamy. Add eggs, one at a time, until combined. Add sifted flour, lemon juice, vanilla and almond extract. Pour mixture into a greased and floured bundt pan. Bake for 1 hour or until a toothpick inserted in the center comes out clean.

Variation: For a richer pound cake, mix in ½ cup sour cream.

Miss Mable's Tea Room
Dickson, Tennessee

Rhubarb Cake

½ C. plus 4 T. butter,
  softened, divided
2 C. sugar, divided
1 egg
2¼ C. flour, divided
1 tsp. baking powder
½ tsp. baking soda

½ tsp. salt
1 C. buttermilk
2 C. fresh or frozen rhubarb,
  thawed
½ C. half n' half
1 tsp. vanilla

Preheat oven to 350°. In a large bowl, combine 2 tablespoons butter and 1 cup sugar. Beat in egg. In a medium bowl, combine 2 cups flour, baking powder, baking soda and salt. Add to sugar mixture, alternating with buttermilk. Beat just until moistened. Fold in rhubarb. Pour batter into a greased 9 x 9″ baking dish. In a separate bowl, combine remaining ¼ cup flour, ¼ cup sugar and 2 tablespoons melted butter. Mix well and sprinkle over batter in pan. Bake for 40 to 45 minutes or until a toothpick inserted in center comes out clean. To make sauce, in a small saucepan over low medium heat, melt remaining ½ cup butter. Add remaining ¾ cup sugar and half n' half. Bring to a boil. Boil 2 to 3 minutes, until thickened. Stir in vanilla. Remove cake from oven. Let cool slightly before cutting into squares. To serve, spoon sauce over warm cake.

Lynn's Country Tea Place
Waverly, Iowa

Dundee Cake

1 C. butter, softened
1 C. sugar
5 eggs
½ C. blanched almonds
2½ C. flour, sifted
½ tsp. baking powder
½ tsp. salt
1 C. golden raisins

1 C. currants
½ C. mixed candied fruit
1 T. grated orange peel
2 T. orange juice
Almond halves
Strips of citron
Candied cherries

Preheat oven to 300°. In a medium bowl, cream together butter and sugar. Beat in eggs, one at a time. Grind almonds and add to batter. Into a separate bowl, sift flour, baking powder and salt. Add raisins, currants and mixed candied fruit to flour mixture. Add to batter and mix well. Stir in grated orange peel and orange juice. Pour batter into a greased 9″ tube pan. Decorate top of cake with almond halves, strips of citron and candied cherries. Bake for 1 hour and 15 minutes.

MacNab's Tea Room
Boothbay, Maine

Italian Cream Cake

Makes 16 servings

¾ C. margarine, softened, divided

½ C. shortening

2 C. sugar

5 eggs, separated

2 C. flour

1 tsp. baking soda

1 C. buttermilk

2 tsp. vanilla, divided

1 small pkg. shredded coconut

1 C. chopped pecans

1 (8 oz.) pkg. cream cheese, softened

2¾ C. powdered sugar

Preheat oven to 350°. In a large bowl, cream together ½ cup margarine and shortening. Beat in sugar and egg yolks, one at a time, beating well after each addition. Mix in flour and baking soda, alternating with buttermilk, beating well after each addition. Stir in 1 teaspoon vanilla, shredded coconut and chopped pecans. In a medium bowl, beat egg whites until stiff. Fold egg whites into mixture. Pour batter into 3 greased and floured 8″ square cake pans. Bake for 25 minutes or until a toothpick inserted in center comes out clean. In a separate bowl, beat together remaining ¼ cup margarine and cream cheese. Add powdered sugar and remaining 1 teaspoon vanilla, beating until smooth. Remove cakes from oven and let cool. To prepare, gently remove cakes from pan and place 1 cake on serving platter. Spread an even layer of cream cheese mixture over cake. Top with another cake, spread with cream cheese and top with final cake. Spread remaining cream cheese mixture over top and sides of cake. If desired, garnish with additional chopped pecans.

Joie De Vie Tea Salon
Des Moines, Iowa

Tropical Cake

1 box lemon cake mix
1 (8 oz.) can crushed
   pineapple in syrup
1 T. cornstarch
¼ C. sugar

1 (8 oz.) container whipped
   topping
Shredded coconut
   for garnish

Bake cake according to box instructions, using two 8″ or 9″ round pans. Remove from oven and let cool. Meanwhile, in a small saucepan, combine crushed pineapple in syrup, cornstarch and sugar. Bring to a boil and let cool. Place one cake onto serving plate and spread pineapple mixture on top. Top with other cake. Spread whipped topping over entire cake. Sprinkle with shredded coconut and serve.

Tea Tyme & What Nots
Fredericksburg, Virginia

Tea Room Contributors

**Chantilly Tea Room
& Gift Boutique**
Tucson, Arizona
520-622-3303

**An Afternoon to Remember –
Tea Parlor and Gifts**
Newcastle, California
916-663-6358

Chado Tearoom
Pasadena, California
626-431-2832

Elise's Tea Room
Long Beach, California
562-424-2134

Kaleidoscope Inn & Gardens
Nipomo, California
866-504-5444

**Rose Mountain Manor
B&B and Tea Room**
Colfax, California
866-444-ROSE

The Gilded Rose Manor
Northridge, California
818-831-0511

Boulder Dushanbe Teahouse
Boulder, Colorado
303-442-4993

Tranquili-tea Tea Room
Denver, Colorado
303-320-1106

**The Front Parlour Tearoom
at The British Shoppe**
Madison, Connecticut
800-842-6674

White Lilac Tearoom
Stratford, Connecticut
203-378-7160

Magnolia & Ivy
Sandestin, Florida
850-267-2595

**Tastefully British Shop
and Tea Room**
Sarasota, Florida
941-927-2612

The Little Café & Tea Shoppe
Jupiter, Florida
561-630-4044

Aion Antiquities & Tea House
Chicago, Illinois
773-489-1534

Jefferson Hill Tea Room
Naperville, Illinois
630-420-8521

The Great Galena Peddlery
Galena, Illinois
815-777-2307

Joie De Vie Tea Salon
Des Moines, Iowa
515-491-0593

Lynn's Country Tea Place
Waverly, Iowa
319-882-4732

**The Rose Cottage Gift Shop
& Tea Room**
Clear Lake, Iowa
641-357-6400

The Glenwood Village & Tearoom
Shreveport, Louisiana
318-868-3652

MacNab's Tea Room
Boothbay, Maine
800-884-7222

Retro Tea Room
Bowie, Maryland
301-262-2274

Brewster Teapot
at the Beechcroft Inn
Brewster, Massachusetts
508-896-9534

Christine's B&B and Tea Room
Great Barrington/Housatonic
Massachusetts
800-536-1186

Mullen's Herbal Tea House
Barre, Massachusetts
978-355-2157

The Wenham Tea House
and Shops
Wehnam, Massachusetts
978-468-1235

British Pantry & Tea Garden Café
Tecumseh, Michigan
517-423-7873

Aprille's Showers Tea Room
Farmington, Minnesota
651-460-2000

Tale of Two Sisters Tearoom
& Gift Shoppe
Red Wing, Minnesota
651-388-2250

The Main Street Mill
Historic Tea Room
Smithville, Missouri
816-532-8377

the shoppe at Shady Gables
Authentic English Tearoom
and Gift Gallery
Versailles, Missouri
573-378-2740

Lady Caroline's British Tea Shop
Omaha, Nebraska
402-551-4TEA

Belle's Tea Cottage
Reno, Nevada
775-826-3006

The Mountain Tearooms
Long Valley, New Jersey
908-876-4626

Alice's Tea Cup
New York City, New York
212-799-3006

Franchia Tea
New York City, New York
212-213-2527

Miss Ruby's Tea Room
Lexington, North Carolina
336-224-2795

Sheffield's Tea Room
Wallace, North Carolina
910-285-8600

Swan House Tea Room & Shoppe
Findlay, Ohio
419-429-7926

A Spot For Tea
Oklahoma City, Oklahoma
405-720-2765

A Perfect Blend
Lititz, Pennsylvania
717-627-4707

Miss Mable's Tea Room
Dickson, Tennessee
615-441-6658

Tea Tyme & What Nots
Fredericksburg, Virginia
540-368-0675

Elizabeth and Alexander's
English Tea Room
Bothell, Washington
425-489-9210

The Secret Garden Tea Room
Sumner, Washington
253-826-4479

Index

Sauces & Snacks

Breads & Sides

Main Dishes & Soups

Desserts